END OF DAYS

ETHICS, TRADITION, AND POWER IN ISRAEL

NEW PERSPECTIVES IN POST-RABBINIC JUDAISM

Series Editor
Shaul Magid (Indiana University, Bloomington)

For more information on this series, please visit:
academicstudiespress.com/newperspectives

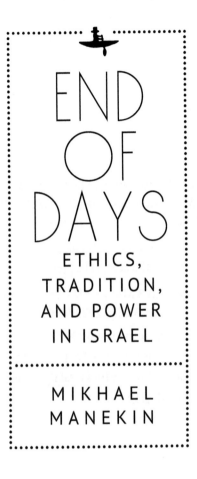

END OF DAYS

ETHICS, TRADITION, AND POWER IN ISRAEL

MIKHAEL MANEKIN

Translated from Hebrew
by Maya Rosen

BOSTON
2023

Library of Congress Cataloging-in-Publication Data

Names: Manekin, Mikhael, author. | Rosen, Maya, translator.

Title: End of days ethics, tradition, and power in Israel / Mikhael Manekin; translated by Maya Rosen.

Other titles: Atḥalta. English

Description: Boston : Academic Studies Press, 2023. | Series: New perspectives in post-rabbinic Judaism

Identifiers: LCCN 2023027369 (print) | LCCN 2023027370 (ebook) | ISBN 9798887193236 (hardback) | ISBN 9798887193243 (paperback) | ISBN 9798887193250 (adobe pdf) | ISBN 9798887193267 (epub)

Subjects: LCSH: Arab-Israeli conflict--Religious aspects--Judaism. | Arab-Israeli conflict--Moral and ethical aspects. | Jewish ethics--Political aspects.

Classification: LCC BM538.P3 M3613 2023 (print) | LCC BM538.P3 (ebook) | DDC 296.3/8--dc23/eng/20230626

LC record available at https://lccn.loc.gov/2023027369

LC ebook record available at https://lccn.loc.gov/2023027370

ISBN 9798887193236 (hardback)
ISBN 9798887193243 (paperback)
ISBN 9798887193250 (adobe pdf)
ISBN 9798887193267 (epub)

Book design by Kryon Publishing Services
Cover by Ivan Grave
Published by Academic Studies Press
1577 Beacon Street
Brookline, MA 02446, USA
press@academicstudiespress.com
www.academicstudiespress.com

To Yael

Contents

Preface

End of Days is an Israeli story. It is also a Jewish story. In some ways it is an Israeli story that struggles to find its Jewish story. A story of power that struggles with ethics. A story of homeland that struggles with Diaspora. A story of survival that struggles with compassion.

For many Diaspora Jews, the story may seem incongruous. It begins with an experience in the IDF where a young idealistic soldier is horrified by humiliating an elderly Palestinian woman. It is a story that many American Jews, who largely valorize and romanticize the IDF, would find odd or even dissonant, but for most Israeli Jews it is all too commonplace.

How can one born into the Zionist story, born into the story of the *novum* of Jewish history, question its legitimacy? In some ways, Manekin's life and memoir weave together the multiple layers of that very historical moment. He is born of an Israeli mother and an American father, both of whom are academics in an American university and shuttle between Israel and the US. A centerpiece of his story is the maternal grandfather he never met but after whom he is named, a simple Jew who survived the war and immigrated to Palestine, and then Israel, who embodied for Manekin the ethics of the Diaspora, that is, Judaism, in the new untested project of Jewish sovereignty and power.

Manekin inherits that struggle in a different era. His life is not fighting for survival against the Nazi genocide, but making sense of power that humiliates those he rules over. From victim to hegemon, from Diaspora to homeland, from a reader of classical Jewish texts to one who holds a gun and threatens civilians under his command. So many Jews in the Diaspora, and Israel, celebrate that newly found power, are even inebriated by it. Manekin is not one of them. He lives in it and he is wounded and terrified by it. This is a story full of contrasts and contradictions. His story embodies an Israeli generation, some of whom can seriously ask the question, "Was Zionism worth it?"

In the 1970s and 1980s, especially after the election of Menachem Begin and the Likud party in 1977, Jewish thinkers began to seriously ponder the question of Jewish power. The challenge, they suggested, after the exuberance of survival and statehood, was how Jews would navigate power after being powerless for so long. Figures such as Irving (Yitz) Greenberg, David Hartman, Emil Fackenheim, and many others wrote about power as the true challenge of the Zionist project. In a rare interview sometime in the 1960s, Rav Soloveitchik asked the same question. The iconoclastic Israeli scientist Yeshayahu Leibowitz warned his listeners that there is nothing stopping Israel from becoming a modern-day Pharaoh. Few listened. Negotiating power was not a foregone conclusion, and in those heady days in the '70s and '80s it became the *sine qua non* of many Zionists, especially but not exclusively religious Zionists, raised in the triumphalism of Rav Kook's ideology and the sustained belief that the victory in 1967 was an act of divine intervention. A certainty set into the Israel narrative post-'67 that was enthusiastic, and dangerous. In the beginning, the former pervaded over the latter and sadly that remains true for many today. For people like Manekin, it is reversed. The power that was once celebrated as a divine gift is now the power that threatens to destroy the Zionist story.

A friend reminded me during a conversation about why we are still reading Greenberg and Hartman's essays on Jewish power that, when they wrote their essays in the late 1970s, they were closer to Auschwitz then they are to us today. It was, for me, an illuminating moment. And yet, as we know, certainly in America, some of those essays are read as if they are still relevant today, over forty years later, after half a century of brutal occupation. *End of Days* comes to tell us that battle about Jewish power has been lost. We have not risen to the occasion of maintaining a sense of ethics in light of power. The world of Manekin's grandfather, who came to Palestine expecting to build an ethical nation, failed. We have become, as the Zionist adage goes, "like all the nations," but not in a good way.

In a way, Manekin's *End of Days* comes to tell a story after the failure of the project of power; after the optimism of the Greenbergs and Hartmans and Fackenheims produced the brutality of a chauvinism with a level of force that terrifies those like Manekin, who hold to a memory of a generation he did not know but sought to emulate nonetheless, even if that generation was somewhat mythologized. Opposing an apologetics of the necessity of such brutality and refusing to simply conclude that Zionism, in effect, was not worth that price, *End of Days* offers a deep immanent critique of a religious Zionism, and liberal Zionism, that Manekin cannot abandon but cannot justify. His choice to remain inside the world whose veil he rips off in anger, shame, and honesty both makes the story compelling and frustrating at the same time. And thus, worth reading.

End of Days is not a work of ideology or political theology. It does not offer solutions to a dilemma that may have no solution. It is the story of a deeply committed Jew with both feet in his homeland and a commitment to the tradition, who simply can no longer tolerate outdated excuses and justifications for the brutality of the state. And he cannot extricate himself from the specter of his grandfather, the Diaspora Zionist who came as a refugee and then became a kind of stranger in the land that saved him. The "48 Generation," as they are called, fought for survival and to be liberated from foreign power. They gained their freedom, which then led to an idealistic young man like Manekin finding himself fully armed and in the position of humiliating a Palestinian woman on her property.

In an essay right before the founding of the state, Hannah Arendt argued against its immediate establishment, because she felt that taking traumatized people and arming them to rule over others who view them as an enemy would never work. But the Zionists scoffed at her pessimism and the world needed to solve a refugee crisis. The state was formed. But Arendt was right. And in Manekin's generation, two generations removed from that horrific genocide, the reality of victimhood has become so embedded in the collective psyche that questioning it brings the accusation of treason. Antisemitism has become Israel's foreign policy and even raison d'etre, and thus ethics has slowly disappeared and viewed as a luxury for the comfortable Tel Aviv "liberals." Certainly not for all, and not for Manekin; but telling that story as personally and as brilliantly as he does comes at a price. If you do not justify or advocate for domination, you are a traitor to the cause.

Manekin's grandfather was a "simple Jew," but Manekin's inheritance is far more complex. His mother is a historian and his father a philosopher, and so Manekin must think his way through this morass called contemporary Israel with a historian's sensibility and care for detail and a philosopher's eye for contradiction. The ideological world that surrounds Manekin's generation is a complex swirl of romanticism, mysticism, pragmatism, hubris, and anger. Sadly, it does not produce a society that can see their own victimhood through the eyes of those who are victimized by them. Rather, too often Zionism constructs a series of justifications that enable survivalism to overshadow political responsibility.

To an extent, *End of Days* tells the story of a lost cause, but in that story lies a belief that somehow Israelis and Jews, Israelis *as* Jews, can move past the survivalism that poisons the well of creating an ethical society, not just *for* Jews, but *of* Jews and others, for all who live under the aegis of the state. Manekin's choice to remain a part of the Israeli project, although he may have moved beyond the Zionist project, is not built on ideological foundations, but is closer to the simplicity of his grandfather. It is an existential posture: "this is where I live, this is my homeland, this is where I am raising my children." In the noise, rancor, and righteous indignation of a people caught in the net of often clever and sometimes banal justification, Manekin walks through the world looking for his grandfather and what he represented. But his grandfather's world and dream are long gone, in part because they were born in the Diaspora. They embodied the Diaspora. This country was created, in part, so his grandfather could live, but what his grandfather stood for seems to have disappeared.

To be clear, this is no romantic pollyannish project of nostalgia. *End of Days* is not a nostalgic book, but it is a hopeful book. Manekin continues to believe, even against his better judgement, in the possibility of a different Israel, and therefore he remains in a world that seems to consistently disappoint him. The question now is not "What will Jews do with power?" That was a question for the 1980s, and sadly that question has been answered. The question now is "What will Jews do with their *abuse* of power?" *End of Days* does not give us the answer. But it forcefully and passionately, and without apology, compels us to ask the question.

Shaul Magid
Cambridge, Massachusetts

Introduction

When I was growing up, if I fought with a kid at school and came home angry, my father would remind me of the Talmudic maxim as cited by medieval Jewish philosopher Maimonides (*Mishneh Torah, Laws of Ethical Behavior* 5:13): "better to be of the offended and not the offender."[1] You don't always have to respond, and you don't have to be aggressive. My father loves this saying, and I would hear it often. One time he joked, "this saying will make you a great Jew but a poor Israeli."

This contradiction—that the virtues supposed to guide the "good" Jew are considered vices for the "good" Israeli is at the center of this book. I wanted to examine our traditional Jewish virtues and their relation to civic virtues, and particularly those virtues expected from Israeli citizens.

Discussion regarding the inability to reconcile religious and secular virtues is not new. It is undoubtedly not unique to Israel. In the past, religious Jewish Israelis wrote about this issue extensively. Yet examinations of this topic from a spiritual perspective become few in recent decades. The results are tragic, both for the state and for religion. Without serious contemplation, religious and secular virtues are confused with each other. As a result, many believe that a religious Jew must be a hyper-nationalist Jew. Nothing could be further from the truth.

My entrance into this conversation is not academic. I have had the incredible good fortune of being able to devote myself to anti-occupation activism for most of my adult life. My ethical worldview, which frames my activism, is rooted in my spiritual education. The duty of asking myself, "What good do I need to do?," always brings me back to my religious roots. Yet the kippa on my head raises questions among fellow activists: "How do you reconcile your religious and political worldviews?" Sadly, this question is asked not only by secular but also by religious friends. Again and again, I need to explain that the gap is nonexistent and that Jewish ethics inform my politics. If anything, the gap lies elsewhere—between the Israeli understanding of legitimate force and my Jewish upbringing. This book is an attempt to engage with this gap.

---

1   Moses Maimonides, *Mishneh Torah* (Jerusalem: Vaghsal Publishing, 1990), 95. Hebrew.

A note to my English-speaking readers: naturally, conversations about politics happen in specific contexts. The American, and particularly the American Jewish conversation, is contextualized differently for various social, political, and historical reasons. The American discussion often focuses on ideologies, viewing Israel as a fight between multiple coherent values. From an internal perspective, things are much messier.

Let me state the point as clearly as possible: this book is not a "Zionist" book, nor is it "anti-Zionist" or "post-Zionist." I am not interested in presenting a perfect moral structure for state behavior, nor am I conversely interested in arguing that Jewish nationalist systems are automatically and inherently corrupt. That ideological conversation is important, but it sometimes doesn't allow for other no less critical conversations—such as how an individual or community should create and engage politically within a broken national framework. Those who believe that the national political context, because it is either pure good or pure evil, negates personal and communal questions might have a challenging time reading this book. I do, however, invite readers to understand the complexities and challenges of reconciling (and sometimes separating) the individual and the national. Not only does that separation allow us to understand our political contexts deeply, but they also help us act in troubled times.

Acknowledgments

I am, first and foremost, a grassroots activist. The patience needed to write is completely foreign to my temperament and training. To compensate, many friends and partners came to my assistance. First, I want to thank Oded Naaman, who wrote this book with me to a great extent. He challenged and added to every argument, and I thank him greatly. Second, I thank Jason Rogoff, who studied all the religious sources with me to enable me to be fair with those I chose to debate. Third, I thank my Hebrew editor, Motty Fogel, who reviewed every argument, looked for inconsistencies in my logic, and helped me be precise. In addition to their professional work, all three are close friends and even closer after the writing process. For their patience, I thank them sincerely.

I've been very fortunate to be surrounded by friends who read, contributed their ideas, argued, and helped me focus: Maya Rosen for her translation, Shai Agmon, Gabriel Ebenzur, Nasreen Hadad Haj Yahya, Brit Yaakobi, Efrat Yerday, Hallel Baitner, Sharon Shahaf, Aviad Huminer, Eli Bitan, Lital Kaplan, Fkade Ababeh, Daniel May, Amir Engel, and of course Samer Swaid, who agreed to be interviewed for the book. I would also like to thank Shaul Magid for all of his help with the English version of this book. Thank you.

My parents, Charles and Rachel, played a significant role in this book. The phrase in Proverbs, "Hear, my son, the instruction of thy father, and forsake not the teaching of thy mother," was written about them. My mother agreed to tell stories of her childhood and her father, and to pass her teachings to me. She read drafts to make sure I am exact as possible. I owe the coherence of this book to my father's education and instruction. We sometimes perceive a lack of compromise and a strong moral compass as contradictory to warmth and kindness, but my father proves the opposite.

To my wife, Yael: to thank you for reading every thought in and draft of the book, for revising and refining, for erasing and expanding, and for translating my grandfather's Yiddish letters to Hebrew would be far too little. This is, of course, true, but it minimizes my thanks for a series of actions. I have molded my life and identity over almost two decades jointly with you. For your continued willingness to be my partner, I am endlessly grateful.

Lastly, to our children—Ruth, Sarai, and Noach: your curiosity, excitement, and love for our family and community fill us with joy daily. Your presence in our life helps us distinguish between what is important and what isn't, what is right and what is wrong. While it might take some years until you read this, I want to end with a direct thought for you:

> We try to create a home protecting you from the world's hardships. Yet we realize that it is an increasing challenge to bridge the gap between the ethics of our home and those of Israel. The ever-growing contradictions and confusions sometimes take a toll and make you pay a price. Our insistence on raising you similarly to how we were raised does not stem from a desire to strengthen you, but rather from a great love for you and the spiritual world to which we belong. I believe that when you are old enough, this book will help you better understand yourselves. You are and always have been our primary audience.

Your grandfather, my father, likes to say that the problem with Religious Zionists is that they read Maimonides's Mishneh Torah from the back to the front; they start with the chapters on the politics of kings and redemption instead of starting the beginning, with the ethics of the individual Jew. Please see this book as a tool to help you read our tradition in the right order.

1

Remembering

"God said to Moses: Write this in a document as a reminder and instill it in Joshua's ears." The Holy Blessed One admonished Moses, who was the rabbi of Israel, to write because writing greatly benefits memory. And if the Holy Blessed One admonished Moses, our teacher, to write, how much more must other people constantly ponder and examine their actions, lest they sin. Therefore, people should write down their sins so that they have a reminder by which they can correct their wrongs, or if they find in a book a way to repent for their sins, they should write it down on a piece of paper immediately, so that they can correct it, without delay, to the extent possible.

—Tzvi Hirsch Kaidenover, *Kav HaYashar* (Poland, seventeenth century)[1]

Prologue

It happened in the year 2000, though I don't remember the exact date. I remember that it was around the time of the holiday of Purim, and I remember the equipment that I was wearing and that I carried with me. I wore layers of clothing, either against the cold or for my protection: boots, a shirt, and pants, a battle vest, a padded coverall, thermal socks, gloves, and a helmet. I carried with me at all times an M16 equipped with devices for night vision, a small walkie-talkie that would always fall out of my vest pocket, cartridges, two military water bottles, and some candy that I kept in my vest to pass the time and with which to console myself about my homesickness.

I served as an infantry officer in the Golani Brigade, and we were stationed in the village of Salim in the West Bank. Before we arrived in Salim, the area commander had warned us that it was "a hornet's nest of terrorists." Salim

---

1   Tzvi Hirsch Kaidenover, *Kav Hayashar* (Jerusalem: Ktav Institute, 1982), 130. All references are to Hebrew sources, unless otherwise noted, although titles of articles and chapters in books have been translated into English.

is located right under Mount Ebal—the same mythic mountain on which Joshua wrote a copy of the Torah after conquering the Land of Israel. The area commander compared Mount Ebal to the Beaufort in Lebanon, a mountain in Southern Lebanon, which we knew from Israel's occupation of the area that had ended months earlier. The comparison to Beaufort was meant to demonstrate the danger to us—combatants who had not long ago fought in the remote north. Mount Ebal was always on the horizon above us, a reminder that we were in a threatening war zone, loaded with traditional symbols that had been emptied of their meanings so that there would be room for daily threats: "Snipers at a record high," "IEDs on the side of the road," "Terrorist cells." "In this village," the area commander explained, "if you're not careful, you die. It looks like a typical village, but there are snipers everywhere." Our assignment was to guard the road that led to the nearby Jewish settlement of Elon Moreh—constructed on the land where Jews believe Abraham built an altar on his travels after leaving Haran according to God's directive.

Our role was largely mundane: ensuring that Palestinian farmers did not cross the road which was meant for Jewish settlers only. The fear was that Palestinian terrorists would leave mines along the route. But the road separated the village from its surrounding agricultural land, and so Salim's villagers would try daily to cross the road with their flocks of sheep. We were at the beginning of a violent intifada that we did not understand and which was, at the time, characterized by roadside bombs. Explosive devices and shootings were common here, whether against us or against those Israeli citizens who had come to fulfill God's promise to Abraham.

To monitor the road, we took over a Palestinian house on the outskirts of the village and stationed soldiers at the windows. An additional force was on radio standby, ready to approach any shepherd or terrorist who got too close to the road. The house belonged to a Palestinian family which was unlucky enough to have a home in a position that suited our assignment. Their building became our new temporary base. The family moved out to live in the house next door, a few meters from us. I remember several generations living together—a grandmother, parents, and children—but I don't know how many people or how old they were. The experience was new to me, and I tried to make sense of this military reality, searching for ad hoc justifications. I remember a conversation with my father about the halakhic question of whether one may forcibly remove people from their homes for the sake of protecting lives. I indeed lived in "a dangerous hornet's nest," but I was a young officer, tired and confused. I knew that I probably would not be a heroic commander like Erez Gerstein, the legendary Golani Brigade commander who had been killed a year before in Southern Lebanon and who we all idealized; I had to do my job well and hoped that the time passed quickly.

During this time, I was pretty burned out, as far as I can remember. I didn't read much, and I didn't think much. It had only been a year since I had left my religious seminary, my yeshiva, but that life felt very distant. I sometimes spoke with rabbis from the yeshiva, especially during difficult times. Still, the conversations generally revolved around me, the military reality around me, and about how long I could survive there before requesting to be transferred to a different unit. We did not speak about Torah. Most of my focus was pursuing my daily tasks, and I used the little energy I had to ensure that my soldiers carried out their tasks and did not themselves go AWOL. Once, one of my soldiers, exhausted from patrols and guard duty, left the base, boarded a bus, and headed for his home. I got on the bus after him, trying to convince him to return, until we got to the nearby settlement of Ariel. I slowly convinced him to stay and we returned, both of us feeling defeated, to the house.

Our routine did not last long, maybe a few months, but I remember it as an eternity. I barely recognized myself during those months; I was always tired. We lived in the house for a few consecutive weeks. I stank all the time—from indifference and constantly being on alert. I slept in an unzipped sleeping bag without taking off my boots, in case I was awakened to deal with terrorists on the "route"—which is what we called the road. Usually, I was woken up to manage the daily struggle against the Palestinian farmers trying to reach their land.

To those around me, everything seemed fine. I was a good soldier, even if pensive. I successfully fulfilled my responsibilities. I tried to act humanely and assertively. These were violent days. Five platoon commanders from my officer training course were killed during the Second Intifada, serving all over the West Bank and Gaza. There were attacks close to my home in Jerusalem and other cities in Israel. We used our guns often, controlling many Palestinians' lives and movements. I didn't speak up often, neither to the Palestinians under my control nor the soldiers under my orders. I felt that I was doing my job. I assume that there were thousands of soldiers and officers like me at that same time in different areas. The situation I was in, just like my mood and my behavior, was in no way exceptional.

One day, I stepped outside the house serving as our makeshift base. I had to pee, and with all due respect to the "hornet's nest" that was this village, there was no functional bathroom in the house in which we slept. Every soldier knows that routine overcomes any fear or sense of danger. I had to urinate, and the grass outside was more inviting than the broken bathroom inside. I pulled down my pants, and when I glanced up, I saw the older woman whose home we had taken and who was now living in the house next door. I saw her, and I saw that she saw me. There were maybe fifteen feet between us—no more than that. Suddenly, she was in front of me; she existed, and I was naked. I had not intentionally pulled my pants down in front of her; I just did not seen her.

She looked at me. Her gaze was not one of embarrassment but rather of contempt and disgust. My coarse behavior did not embarrass her. Why would it? I lived in her home against her will. I had taken her home by force. Now, standing exposed before her, I was a savage. I disgusted her. I always wear a kippa, and I was wearing one then. The woman couldn't see it—my helmet concealed it—but I knew the kippa was there. I understood that I transgressed. I had not transgressed intentionally, but I should have seen the woman and paid attention to her presence before lowering my pants. If there was one moment in my life at which I knew in a single instance, as clear as day, that I was desecrating God's name, it then. Although I served in the army for about another year and a half afterward, and I was frequently numb, at that particular moment—when I was revealed in my baseness, focused only on myself in sight of the woman whom I had expelled from her home—I knew with certainty that I had desecrated God's name. I would not have understood the significance of this moment without my traditional Jewish upbringing. But my memory was too weak, and understanding came only after the deed.

The Letter, Part 1

Haifa Immigrant Camp, end of 1949

Simcha,

. . . Night. The ship slowly glides across the water's surface towards the Land of Israel. Everything is too slow. It becomes clear that the captain is delaying bringing the ship, which carries 1,700 Jews, into port until daylight. Here—the sun starts to rise. "And there was light." Before our eyes, the hope of seventy-two generations reveals itself in all of its glory—the mountains of Zion. I stand as if bound to the ship's railing as it approaches the port—the tension peaks. The eyes, the heart, one's entire essence is bound up in this great revelation. My whole being is shaking. My heart is beating quickly. I stare at the great, naked hills in front of us. They are the first to welcome us.

Miraculously, I see an old, gray man with a long cane walking with his elderly wife. They stroll at the top of the hill, talking with each other about a worldly matter. Who could it possibly be? I look carefully. Oy! It is our old grandfather

Abraham with Sarah. They are walking to Gerar, the home of Avimelech, king of the Philistines. Abraham asks of his wife Sarah, "Please say that you are my sister, so that it will go well for me because of you, and that I will live because of you." The story from the Torah took place on the land which my eyes see.

I strain my eyes and see a second image, even more extraordinary. A small group of children leading a flock of sheep and goats "streaked, speckled, and mottled." A great herd led by slaves and maidservants, our ancient father, leading them. I push myself hard against the railing of the ship to see.

[...]

Here you are, dear mother of Zion! The mother of our past, the mother of our present, and the mother of our future. You see, you are our beloved mother. Not a skyscraper of a young woman like in America, but a sort of sweet, elderly grandmother with thin, wrinkled hands, dried out from two thousand years of longing for the children whom the evil Titus banished. This is how you look now, as your children gather like birds from the four corners of the earth. You stand, mother, thin, maternal hands with the strength and vivaciousness of youth. Every boat and every airplane brings your children to you, and you embrace them in your arms and cry out in great joy, "My children, my children, every one of you. You see once again the nation and your liberated land."

My dreams reached their highest heights. I was moved to tears. I could not stop the tears in my eyes, and I let them flow into the sea. There were many reasons for these tears, primarily the joy of "the children shall return to their land," but also the sadness of the burnt ashes of my father, my mother, and our brothers and sisters. Their ashes were carried by the wind, lost in the world perhaps not far from the ship, somewhere, who knows where.

[...]

At about 6:00 am, the ship reached the Haifa port. We were surrounded by noise and commotion from all sorts of boats—big and small, and even bigger, like giant blocks. The ships are run by Jewish captains, like the mighty Samson. I stand with groggy eyes and look at these big people, how everything is happening so quickly. A miracle happened for us in such a short period, after Treblinka, after Auschwitz, and after Exodus, when the British guard ships would surround the boats and not let them pass, and now . . . now, we finally arrive.

(Written by my grandfather, Yehiel Mikhael Becher, upon his arrival in the Land of Israel in 1949, translated from Yiddish by Yael Levi)

How to Be a Jew in the State of Israel

In recent years, I have been consumed by the question of how to be a Jew in Israel. This is an ostensibly strange question with an easy answer. Israel is the "State of the Jews," and according to many, it is also the "Jewish State." To be a Jew in Israel, one must simply be a Jew who lives here, in Israel. Most citizens here are Jews. Public life is full of Jewish symbols, Jewish public figures, and different public displays of Jewish ethics. The state is so "Jewish" that there have been fierce debates in recent years regarding "excessive" Jewishness in the public sphere and about the religious coercion of nonreligious people. It often feels that Judaism chases you down in Israel, even when you attempt to evade it.

But even so, I am overwhelmed and ashamed. I don't want Judaism to be an automatic extension of my being here. I want to live my Judaism actively and with intention. So I close my eyes and try to imagine the Jew I aspire to be. I see a person committed to divine truth, a gentle person, reflective and compassionate, who recoils from violence and loves other people. I imagine a learned person, attentive and curious, someone who is critical. I imagine a person who believes.

Yet the believing Jew of my imagination is an idealized version from a different time and place and lives in a completely different political context than my own. My imagined Jewish model is from a pre-Israel past, a Jew for whom Jewish identity is not rooted in national pride or sovereignty but rather in humility and compassion. I feel my confusion creeping in: What is the connection between Jewish belief and Jewish ethics, on the one hand, and political power, on the other? Is my imagined Jew a compassionate person and a lover of justice because of religious belief or a lack of power? Does the very fact of my being Israeli mean that I will never be like that Jew, that I am destined to be a different kind of Jew?

My confusion is replaced by a deep sadness when I open my eyes. There are many Jews around me who are proud of their Jewishness, but I have no desire to be like them. They are entirely different from the Jew of my imagination. They pursue power and hesitate for not even a moment in their attempts to achieve it. Instead, they love and are excited by the battlefield.

I live in Israel, love living in Israel, and feel responsible for my surroundings. I do not want to negate my existence here, the presence of other Jews here, or the great power that my people have accumulated in the last decades. But I also do not want to oppose my people's ethical, compassionate tradition. I am angry because the state's power should have served the Jewish people and their way of life, but the Jews instead devoted themselves to power and were tainted by its force. A Jew without power says, "Just as the Holy Blessed One is referred to as merciful, so too must you be merciful." A Jew with power declares, "We must show the Arabs that we run the show here; we must subdue them." I am overwhelmed because Israeli Jewishness commands me to scorn compassion. I am lost between the Judaism of my grandparents, whose values are my own, and the Israeli Judaism of power, from which I feel increasingly alienated.

"Take very great care of yourselves, lest you forget"

Power presents ethical challenges. A person with power is liable to exploit power for wrongdoing, pay no mind to harming others, or view power as a sign of superiority above other people. But for the religious individual, power is dangerous for an additional reason too. Power, and its attendant advantages, is liable to distract religious people from the tradition to which they had cleaved before gaining power. It can lead to ignorance, and ignorance is the enemy of tradition.

We are commanded to remember. We read in Deuteronomy 4:9 that the Holy Blessed One warns the Children of Israel, immediately before they enter the land, "Take utmost care and take very great care of yourselves, lest you forget the things which you saw with your own eyes and lest they fade from your mind as long as you live. Make them known to your children and your children's children[. . . .] Take care, lest you forget the covenant that the Lord your God made with you. Make no sculpted image or any likeness against which God has commanded you." Forgetting God, ignoring our past, leads one to be enslaved to idolatry.

My grandfather arrived in the State of Israel in 1949, one of "the surviving remnant," a small minority of Polish Jews who survived the Holocaust and came to Israel, mostly from refugee camps. The letter quoted above was written three weeks after he arrived in Israel, full of hope for a new religious life.

Despite his happiness about his emigration to Israel, my grandfather's world of references was that of Polish Jewry. When he looked out over the mountains of Carmel, he did not imagine mighty soldiers, nor did he imagine Joshua or King David. He instead envisioned our elderly ancestors, canes in hand, walking with their children. The land was not a young woman but an elderly mother. Coming to Israel was, for my grandfather, a return home. For him, "home" was a combination of his life in a Jewish town in Poland and images of the Land of Zion from Jewish tradition.

My grandfather and I grew up in different places and times. I cannot be "Diasporic," even if I want to be—and I do not want to be. I grew up in Israel, and that is an irreversible fact. I like living in Israel; it is my home. I speak in Hebrew with my children and with my friends. These are not inconsequential matters. Hebrew is a central part of my tradition. I read texts written in Hebrew hundreds of years ago with much greater ease than my grandmothers and grandfathers, for whom Hebrew was not a language they spoke. The Israeli geographic landscape allows me to understand the Jewish calendar and those religious commandments that apply only to Israel's Land.

The State of Israel sees itself as being in a constant state of emergency and perpetual defense, yet in reality, we are powerful. Our state has nuclear arms and one of the strongest armies in the world. Despite its relatively small size, Israel is among the world's developed countries and conducts trade with most of the world's nations. I am a free individual in a sovereign state, and I have the power of a person who lives in a sovereign state, a nontrivial privilege. However, the power that this security grants me is a double-edged sword. "Jewish" justifications—both national and religious—enable both my privileged status as a Jewish citizen and also the most horrendous ways we treat Arabs who live here with us, including, most significantly, our continued control over millions of Palestinians.

An Old Jew in the New Jewish World

Basing our spiritual and political foundations on the ethical behavior of our forefathers is central to our tradition. Doing so requires a conscious decision to actively remember our past, through the lens of our Jewish texts and stories. I choose to remember my grandfather and the traditions he brought with him when he disembarked from the ship in the Haifa port. I choose to remember, and, in doing so, I remain steadfast in my adherence to a religious life that has all but vanished from Israeli public discourse.

Jewish tradition, of course, did not disappear by chance. Zionist leadership in Israel saw the traditional beliefs that my grandfather and others like him held as emblematic of the old order they rebelled against. In an essay entitled "The State of Israel and the Future of the Nation," David Ben-Gurion, the first Prime Minister of Israel, wrote:

If we were to ask a learned Jew two hundred years ago, "what is a Jew?" he would answer simply and self-assuredly: "a Jew is a descendant of our father Abraham, who keeps the commandments and awaits the coming of the Messiah." And such an answer would satisfy Jews around the world. But today, such an answer would no longer satisfy a good number of our people, perhaps the majority. Since the Emancipation and the freeing of human thought from the constraints of tradition, religion has ceased to be the uniting, unifying, and dominant force among much of the Jewish people. It is no longer the case that the inheritance of all Jews includes a connection to the Jewish nation, and not many Jews in our day await the Messiah.[2]

In Ben-Gurion's imagined timeline of the development of the Jewish people, he argues that there were once simple, traditional Jews who were secure in their faith. They kept the commandments and prayed for the coming of the Messiah. These traditional Jews belong to the past. Following both internal and external upheavals, a new kind of Jew arose. Ben-Gurion saw himself as the leader of this more advanced, contemporary form of Judaism. New Jews, he believed, were Jewish pioneers; they were not people who waited passively for the Messiah but people who brought redemption on their own, freed from the old constraints of religion.

This version of history, which separates Jews of the past and Jews of the future, between old Jews of the Diaspora and new Jews of Zionism and redemption, stands at odds with the core of my grandfather's identity: he was an old Jew in a new era. My grandfather was a Jew of "two hundred years ago," in Ben-Gurion's worldview, yet he lived at the same time as Ben-Gurion himself. He was a traditional Jew not only in his personal life; he understood his move to Israel as the realization of a prophetic vision and as the return to a home that had not changed in two thousand years. For my grandfather, the Land of Israel was an old, sweet grandmother who longed for her sons and daughters. Moving to Israel was in keeping with traditional continuity, not opposed to traditions of the past. Unlike many Zionist leaders in those days, my grandfather had no desire to forget or disconnect from his past. Nor did he disdain the lives of Jews who came before him.

2   David Ben-Gurion, "Israel and the Future of our People: The Triangular Bond between Hebrew Culture, State, and Messianic Redemption," *Molad* 15 (date): 107–108, quoted in David Ohana, *Meshiḥiyut U-mamlakhtiyut: Ben-Guryon vVeha-inṭelekṭu'alim Ben Hazon Medini Le-te'ologyah Poliṭit* (Qiryat Sde Boqer: Ben Gurion University 2003), 126.

My grandfather was just one of the hundreds of thousands of Jews who arrived in Israel from Eastern Europe after World War II. In Ben-Gurion's view, their answer to the question "What is a Jew?" was the "premodern" answer, a legacy of the past: a Jew is a descendant of our father Abraham, who keeps the commandments and awaits the coming of the Messiah. Communal traditions inform ethical identity. The disciples of our father Abraham, we learn in the Mishna of Avot 5:19, are endowed with "a good eye, a low spirit, and a humble soul." Maimonides explains that "a good eye means contentment, a low spirit means caution, and a humble soul means humility."[3]

Standing on the deck while the ship entered the Haifa port, my grandfather looked towards Mount Carmel. He thought about his upcoming reunion with our biblical ancestors, the destruction that lay behind him, and the fulfillment of a dream that had survived "seventy-two generations." Yet Ben-Gurion believed that my grandfather's dream had vanished. Ben-Gurion, and with him the dominant narrative in the country, believed that traditional Jewish identity was destined to be wiped out and replaced by a young, rebellious, and new Jewish Israeli identity.

After Forgetting—Lost Traditional Memories in Today's Israel

More than seventy years have passed since the foundation of the State of Israel and my grandfather's arrival in Israel. The model of the new Jewishness has undergone many changes since Ben-Gurion's day; it is no longer the specifically secular-nationalist pioneering formulated by socialist Zionists a decade ago. Today, Ben Gurion's vision of the secular pioneer seems an irrelevant, antiquated relic to many in Israel. Religion, it is said, is on the rise here, and publicly challenging Israel's founding ideology.

The attacks on Ben-Gurion-style secular identity are not only coming from religious leaders and political groups. So-called "secular" quests for a more robust Jewish identity have been on the rise or decades now. Secular learning institutions have opened to foster an "Israeli Judaism" and Jewish values and symbols have become a valuable currency traded in the political system. As a result, the borders of Israeli secularism are being stretched, and with it, the meaning of Israeli Jewishness is changing.

---

3   Moses Maimonides *Perush ha-Rambam le- Avot*, ed. I. Shailat (Maale Edumim: Shailat, 1998), 109 (on *Avot* 5:17, according to Maimonides's numbering).

However, despite the altered course signaled by secular Zionism's attempts at renewal and the growing opposition to the "Ben-Gurion model," there is no sign of a turn towards the traditional world of my grandfather. The "Israeli Judaism" project is aptly named: its leaders seek to create a new Judaism that does not awaken our past traditions. But this Jewish renewal movement (not to be confused with the American Jewish renewal movement) is not alone in averting its gaze from Diasporic religious traditions. It is also—and perhaps primarily—the Religious Zionist movement, which has created an ethical and religious system that denies its past and forsakes our people's traditions. While the Religious Zionist movement's daily practices demand Orthodox observance, the movement simultaneously sanctifies power and sovereignty, presents compassion as weakness, and scoffs at "Diasporic" Judaism. It is somewhat ironic that Religious Zionism follows the path of Ben-Gurion in assuming that Eastern European Judaism is lifeless, powerless, and passive. In contrast to traditional Judaism, Religious Zionism cultivates an aggressive Judaism, using its political power to force its positions and values on nonreligious Jews and other faiths. It also coercively asserts its presence and sovereignty over Arab residents and treats them as visitors who have the fortune to live in the land thanks to our generosity.

Did the State of Israel's Power Destroy Jewish Ethics?

Despite their differences, Religious and secular Zionism both posit that it is necessary to move beyond the communal ethics of our Diasporic past. Both want a new Judaism, an Israeli Judaism. And both want a Judaism which is predicated upon state power while simultaneously bolstering state power. I believe that it is religiously dangerous to accept this type of thinking, to internalize that the era of past Judaism is over, and that maybe I, as a Jew who lives in Israel, don't have access to the world of my grandfather.

The claim that we are in the era of the new Jew merits attention. Conditions of oppression and marginalization formed our forefathers' ethical thinking and practices in the Diaspora. Their political-communal organization was also the outgrowth of this reality. This Jewishness lacked centralized political power and developed in scattered communities under different regimes. Because of this, many Zionists, from the left and from the right, claim that the national political elements of traditional Judaism are those of a minority lacking any real political power and are therefore no longer relevant. Their claim sees an inseparable connection between our national, religious, and political stories. The story that shaped the meaning of life for traditional Jewish communities, which shaped my grandfather's spiritual world, was created in communities that lacked sovereignty. The story that shapes my life is a different one. So are those who seek a new Judaism correct, those who claim that Jewish power undermines traditional Judaism and that denying this fact entails denying the very reality of our lives?

I did not know my grandfather; he died two weeks before my parents married. As is common in Jewish tradition, I am named after him—Yehiel Mikhael. I learned about his world and who he was primarily from his letters and from my mother's stories. When he wrote the letter above, he was about my age now, in his forties. When he moved to Israel with his wife, my grandmother, they had three small children—like I do today. A mere seventy years seperate his life from mine.

The power I hold as an Israeli citizen stands between me and the world of my grandfather. I cannot, and do not want to, take upon myself the conditions of Jewish life in the past. Yet I believe that I must attempt to understand this world and that I am obligated to remember it. Without recognizing this ethical world, it will undoubtedly be hard to imitate it.

Memory as a Traditional Practice

As children, we learn that Jews must act ethically because they are Jews. This principle stands at the center of Jewish tradition, and much Jewish literature presents ethical conduct as central to the requirement to live a suitable Jewish life. For example, the first tractate in the Tractate of Derech Eretz Zuta [The Way of the Land, or Ethics], a text compiled sometime between 200 and 500 CE states: "The characteristics of a scholar are that he is meek, humble, alert, filled [with a desire for learning], modest, beloved by all, humble to the members of his household and sin-fearing. He judges a man [fairly] according to his deeds, and says 'I have no desire for all the things of this world because this world is not for me.'"

For generations, teachers of Jewish ethics have tried to understand which attributes are desirable and which are negative by examining models from the Jewish past. Abraham, Moses, King David, Jeremiah, Rabbi Akiva, Hillel, rabbinic authorities and pious Jews, patriarchs, matriarchs, and saints—examining their deeds was one of the main ways of understanding how Jews should act. This is validated by the famous verse from Proverbs 1:8, "Hear my son, the teaching of your father, and do not forsake the Torah of your mother" (Proverbs 1:8). One cannot adhere to a tradition while simultaneously negating the ethics of one's past.

Yes, times are different now, but historical circumstances have changed many times in the past. Just like a Pietest living in twelfth-century Germany would study the behavior of the prophet Jeremiah and a mystic living in seventeenth-century Tzfat would learn from King David's repentance, so too is an Israeli Jew obligated to understand the behavior of past Jews in the Diaspora and imitate their ways. While life's circumstances do indeed change, this should not mean erasing the tradition but instead reinterpreting it.

God without a State

Before the era of Jewish Israeli sovereignty, the anchor of the Jewish people was not territorial sovereignty or military power. Rather, traditional Jews saw themselves as members of a large family that accepted only the authority of God. Before and after moving to Israel, my Grandfather Mikhael had a regular, personal connection with God. God was always present. My grandfather would tell my mother that he was lucky that God watched over him and protected him. Despite his difficult life, he believed that he survived because of God's help, not his own strength. For my grandfather, God was both friend and king. When he prayed, my grandfather would cry to God. He wasn't satisfied with the three obligatory daily prayers and came up with additional personal prayers. When my mother was sick as a child, he would whisper prayers to God to protect her from harm. The personal divine providence that he believed in connected him to a community of people who spoke with God. In the absence of a human protector, God protected him.

My grandfather was born before World War I, one of seven children in southeast Poland, in a town on the road between Chelm and Lublin. He was born into a Belz Hasidic family, one of many in the area. His community educated him into a personal connection with God. He learned in cheder (a Jewish communal learning institution for children) until the age of ten when his formal education ended. His schooling gave him the tools to pray and study the Bible, Talmud, and halakhic (legal) literature on his own. Of course, my grandfather's childhood's geographic and political landscape differed significantly from my own. Yet the fluid ideological landscape also differed vastly: families could have children who stayed Hasidim and some that had become Zionists, communists, or liberals, all living under the same roof. As a result, it was possible to move between seemingly contradictory worldviews, and it was possible to take part in different movements simultaneously. It was thus possible for my grandfather to be both a Hasid and a Zionist.

Just as I study my grandfather's life to try and understand for myself how a Jew should behave ethically, so too did my grandfather demand of himself a similar sort of mimetic reflection. For pre-Israel Jews, the entirety of the Torah trained a person not only in faith and deeds but also in ethical behavior. He was a "Hasid" in his communal and sectarian affiliation and a Hasid in the literal meaning of the word in Jewish tradition—a pious person who lives according to ethical and religious rules above and beyond the letter of the law.

From my grandfather's perspective, he never rebelled against the Torah of his mother or his father's teachings. On the contrary, he was a traditionalist and expressed traditionalist values in all his choices. In his Hasidism, Zionism, and character, he lived out the communal Judaism that had developed from the traditions he belonged to. The religious ethics he embodied expressed his orientation to community and Jewish tradition.

Must We Erase Traditional Ethics?

The question of how one should be a Jew in Israel doesn't get asked often in the country. Instead of the question of a traditional Jew—"How should I behave?"—the Israeli Jewish question is: How should a Jewish state behave?

Different questions lead to entirely different, and sometimes contradictory, answers. And although a Jew can ask both of these questions in parallel, it seems that with anything having to do with ethical behavior, the question "How should I behave, as a person and as a Jew?" has been entirely eclipsed by the question "How should the state behave?" However, especially when thinking about using force, disengaging with religious and ethical practice has had a severe impact on religious thought. Moreover, Jewish Israeli sovereignty has meant that ethical ways of thinking about Jewish life, especially *Musar* (virtue ethics) literature, have been essentially forgotten in Jewish thought.

In the virtue ethics book *Tomer Devorah*, we read: "one should make oneself accustomed to bringing the love of other people into his heart, even of wicked people, as if they were his brothers, and more than that until he has fixed in his heart love for all people."[4] In the thirteenth-century mystic Abraham Aboulafia's *Hayei Olam HaBa*, we read, "one should humble oneself before all people, listen to their insults [. . .]. His intentions should be for the sake of heaven. His compassion should be even towards those who hate him, so long

---

4 Moses Cordovero, *Tomer Devorah*, ch. 2 (Jerusalem: Adat Bnei Avraham, 2022), 71.

as they do not hate God."[5] Jewish ethical literature instructs people to distance themselves from material goods as much as possible, sometimes including getting rid of all property.

Can nationalist Israeli Jews imagine themselves loving their enemies and scorning the ownership of land and assets? Can they image ethical Judaism as a contentment with less, self-control, scorn for pride (including national pride), and an avoidance of their militaristic idea of honor? To try and behave according to Jewish tradition, I want to return to the traditional tools for understanding individual conduct within the political reality of the State of Israel today.

Jews without Power

There is a gaping chasm between traditional Judaism and Israeli Judaism, which the fact of sovereignty alone cannot explain. There have also been drastic changes in lifestyle and other conditions. The material circumstances of my life and the security I enjoy are entirely different from the instability of my grandfather's life. And although I do not wish for the difficult life circumstances with which my grandfather contended, I want to understand how a poverty and a fragile environment influenced his religious world. This, too, is an understanding demanded by our ethical literature, such as the abovementioned *Tomer Devorah*.[6]

I know very little about my grandfather's childhood and adolescence. I know that his family lived in poverty until World War II. I know that he married my grandmother Matel between the wars when they were in their late twenties. I know that immediately before the invasion of Poland, they realized what was unfolding and started to move east towards the border with Russia. They left behind what little they had.

Yet there are things I don't and can't know. I know nothing about the experience of being a refugee. My grandfather fled his homeland with his wife and their daughter, his brother, and his wife's father. He left his parents and two unmarried sisters at home. The four of them were murdered by the Nazis—I learned this from testimony documents signed with my grandfather's name that I found in the Yad VaShem database. A prayer book was among the few possessions that my grandparents took east with them. On its pages are beet juice stains from when they made do without kosher wine on. They were

---

5   Abraham Abulafia, *Ḥayyei ha-'olam ha-ba'* (Tel Aviv: Barazani, 2001), 17.

6   Cordovero, *Tomer Devorah*, chs. 8 and 9.

refugees, and the fear of death pursued them from where they fled and awaited them even in the places where they sought refuge.

Although Soviet rule was more tolerable than life had been under German control, my grandfather's family was not satisfied there. They were in constant fear of the authorities, especially of the police. Even years later, they were sure that the NKVD, the all-knowing Russian secret police, was listening to them through the walls.

In the Soviet Union during the war, my grandfather made a living doing odd jobs. Once, while working as a painter, he fell off a roof. I am told that after that he walked slowly, with a slight limp, and his hands behind his back. My mother would say that his slow gait, together with his quiet manner, gave him an aristocratic air. It was the gait of learned people who have time to think about life's big questions. But his walk also expressed something else—an uncontrolled life, full of uncertainty, transience, and vulnerability.

When Matel's father died, my grandfather carried his corpse westwards, at great danger to himself, to bury him in a Jewish cemetery. A Jew needs to be buried in a Jewish cemetery. Matel came from a big city, from Chelm, unlike my grandfather, who was from a village. She was born into a small yet important Hasidic line—Kotzk Hasidism. Unlike my grandfather, she was of distinguished lineage, a seventh-generation descendant of Yaakov Yitzhak Horowitz, known as the Seer of Lublin. Of the Seer, it was said that he could see from one end of the world to the other. He knew how to see from before the destruction of the Temple until after the redemption. It was as if the Seer of Lublin fully embodied the story of Eastern European Jewry. His all-encompassing gaze made him almost crazy, at least according to his disciples. It is told in Hasidic mythology that he would walk around with a handkerchief over his eyes to avoid seeing things that he was forbidden to see. The circumstances of his death are still debated. His disciples say that he fought with angels to hasten the redemption and fell from the balcony of his home. His detractors laughed that he was undoubtedly drunk or committed suicide. The fall did not kill him immediately but paralyzed him. His disciples say he died on Tisha B'av, the day on which, according to tradition, the Messiah is born.

The Kotzk Hasidic sect that my grandmother belonged to was almost entirely obliterated in World War II. The few individuals who survived did not succeed in reviving the Hasidic sect in Israel or in the United States. And while there are memories of the Kotzk sect, and especially of their rabbi and his sharp insights, there is no court. My grandmother's family was also murdered.

Finally, after many years of travel, my grandparents reached Uzbekistan, where they stayed until the end of the war. Their second child was born there, my mother's brother. Until her death, Matel remembered the Uzbekistani women around her fondly; despite the women's poverty, they shared the small amount of rice they had with her family. She used to tell my mother that the women would sit side by side, Jews and Uzbekistanis, pulling lice out of their children's heads and talking, laughing, and crying, as if they spoke the same language and understood each other. It was a bond created by their shared language of suffering.

When the war ended, my grandparents were refugees in a Soviet country that had no interest in them. Like hundreds of thousands of others, they moved via Czechoslovakia to a displaced persons' camp outside of Munich, in the American-controlled area. The American soldiers treated them better than the Russian soldiers, but the family continued to live under the rule of foreign soldiers. They were Polish citizens, their home had been destroyed, and like many others after the war, they waited a long time for the powers that be to decide what to do with them as part of the "repatriation" process. They had no desire or ability to return to Poland; their new home was a refugee camp—a home for people with no home.

Despite this, they found a bit of peace after years of poverty and death, of escape and wandering. Matel would talk with excitement about the chocolate handed out to them in the refugee camp. They would later bring with them to Israel the cooking pot that the UN gave them, along with some blankets, wine cups, and a few other random belongings.

In the refugee camp, alongside other displaced people and despite their homelessness, my grandparents flourished. Was it there that my grandfather became an enthusiastic Zionist, or had he already discovered Zionism before the war? I don't know. However, in this period, he found his ideological home. His Zionist home wasn't of the hegemonic leftwing, secular Zionist variety: those heretical socialists were too far from his traditionalist disposition. He was a kosher butcher, the son of a kosher butcher from Eastern Europe, anchored to a life of Torah. His Zionism was not a rebellion but a continuation of the biblical narrative. I don't know when or how he joined Brit Yeshurun—the religious faction of the right-wing Revisionist movement. My mother explained that the revisionist leader Jabotinsky pulled Eastern European Jews into the Zionist world without asking them to change their traditional Jewish lifestyles. My grandfather organized Zionist activities alongside Torah learning events in the refugee camp. This whole movement has been completely forgotten.

When they were still living in the refugee camp, my grandfather edited the Brit Yeshurun newspaper and was a friend of Rabbi Moshe Bernstein, the head of the movement in the camp. Even within the Zionist political movement, my grandfather saw himself primarily as a man of Torah. In a celebratory article in honor of the third anniversary of the movement's activities, he described his mission as spreading Torah to those Zionists who wanted it. Zionists are also Jews. They need a synagogue, *shiurim*, the offerings of a world of Torah. They were part of the Jewish collective, and some of them had survived for years in death camps and labor camps, fleeing from one place to the next; and they were hungry for Torah. My grandmother became pregnant towards the end of their time in the displaced persons' camp and spent her whole pregnancy there. On the day of the birth, my grandfather was confident it would be another son and was very excited. He went and bought a big fish to celebrate the occasion. My mother was born on that day.

Their flourishing in the camp did not make my grandparents forget the past horrors. They could not forget their former home. From their first moments in the displaced persons' camp, my grandfather was active in the Holocaust survivor organizations searching for family and community members who had been lost. Communal and familial memorial evenings were their social activities. They also kept the booklets published by survivors, photo albums from the camps, and other memories, and brought these with them to Israel. These were hidden in a cupboard on the balcony, and my mother was told not to look at them. Once, when my mother was a child, she snuck into the box and saw a picture of a child carrying a wheelbarrow full of corpses. Her parents scolded her when they found out. The search for family members, which began as soon as the war ended, continued until my grandparents' final days, with meetings of survivors from their communities and visits to Yad VaShem.

While many of my grandparents' friends decided to emigrate to America (they called it "the young lady") following the closure of the displaced persons' camp, my grandfather wanted to return to "the mother"—to his history and his people, the place supposed to offer comfort and calm, his eternal home. This was the wish of a person who wanted to rest with every fiber of his being.

I have no nostalgia for the period in which my grandfather lived, and I have no desire to live his life. I do not want to experience the uncertain flight from one place to the next, a journey that defined his life. It is hard for me even to imagine the anguish he experienced with the loss of his family and the destruction of his world. But precisely because I appreciate the anguished hardships that were his lot, I am moved by his and others' abilities to make ethical-religious decisions out of a desire to live as good Jews. We tend to confuse powerlessness and helplessness. But a person without physical security can and must make ethical decisions, while powerful people can be blind to the implications of their actions and slaves to their power.

Sovereignty and the Desecration of God's Name

In Maimonides's *Laws of Repentance* (1:4), he writes:

> One who desecrates God's name, even though he has repented and Yom Kippur has come, and he holds firm in his repentance, and he has suffered, he is not granted full atonement until he dies. Rather, repentance, Yom Kippur, and suffering suspend punishment, and only death atones, as it says, "It was revealed in my ears by the Lord of Hosts . . . this transgression will not be atoned for until you die."

Desecrating God's name is so severe that only death atones for it. My traditional education, my grandfather's education, was supposed to teach me to have good values. When I stood half-naked in 2000 in front of a woman I had banished from her home, I knew that I had failed. The tradition taught me that the misuse of power is a sin. And despite the circumstances of life in Israel, the Torah of my grandfather had not been wholly forgotten from my life.

My grandfather lived without a state and military power to protect him, but his Torah is my Torah. It can be a counterweight against aggressiveness and nationalism when correctly learned and used. For this purpose, I must draw the tradition from the depth of memory and make it a part of my life's reality.

2

Patience

Every humble person is merciful and patient and learns from all people and judges every person favorably and loves peace and pursues peace and in all dealings strives to fulfill the precept to love one's fellow as oneself.

—Eliyahu ben Avraham Shlomo HaKohen, *Shevet Musar* (Turkey, eighteenth century)[1]

The Letter, Part 2

First Immigration Camp in Ra'anana

I am returning to writing this letter after a break of more than three weeks. I just couldn't find the time. Now, at night, I continue in a tent cluttered with suitcases. The wife and children are asleep. It is humid in the tent during the summer, and the dew creeps in. Around us are many other tents and bunks, housing about 3,000 immigrants, may God protect them. We're in an immigration camp in the city of Ra'anana, next to Tel Aviv. So now I can finish the story of our travels from the previous letter. In the Haifa port, government representatives boarded the ship. They greeted us briefly but warmheartedly. Then people started to disembark from the boat. I was among the first. I stood with my two feet on the earth of the Holy Land of Israel. The blood flowed strangely through my veins. Emotion overtook my body like Rabbi Yehuda HaLevi, who stood upon the Holy Land of Israel, bowing down and kissing the earth, the elderly Mother of Zion. With great intention and spiritual upliftment, I said the *shehecheyanu* blessing.

Stewards helped us with our suitcases, and we entered the port. At that moment, I recalled an article in the *Mapam* [the left United Workers Party] newspaper. The writer describes our supposed suffering as new immigrants

---

1   Elijah ben Solomon, *Shevet Mussar* (Piotrków: Yehoshua Gershon, 1888), 73.

who are given "the cold shower"[2] of the sad reality when he disembarks from the ship. Although I am not a particularly political person, I am one of the thousands of immigrants who received this "cold shower" that the *Mapam* writer described. I'm telling you that his description was an exaggeration. For me and the others, it was fine. Not a "cold shower" and not a hot shower. He was talking nonsense . . . He should go find something better to do with his time.

We had seven suitcases. They asked me what I had in them, and I said what I wanted, and thought to myself, "If you don't believe me, please open up the bags"—but no one asked me to open them, and they let me go on.

They did check the others, joyfully opening bags and parcels. Another Jew stood not far from me, and they told him to open his bags. They opened his first one, and in front of my dazed eyes lay forty pieces of pure silver. They opened the second one, and hidden among all the rags were all sorts of "little" things that I would want to have with us now in the camp. These sorts of "poor" and "wretched" immigrants came with us, and having their bags opened was indeed a "cold shower" for them. They didn't enjoy it. *Nu*, what great travail is it that the State of Israel will enjoy their wealth, which they obtained with ease?

Immigrant Temporary Camp, Ra'anana (One and a Half Months in Israel)

In the immigrant camp, everyone was housed, some in huts and some in tents. Everyone received a bed, mattress, blanket, pillow, sheets, and a kettle. First thing, people went to the nearby washing area. They washed and then went to eat. There are no problems with the food; it's delicious. I'll describe the food area: as much fresh white bread as you want, tasty soup, buckwheat cooked with beans, and oranges, a piece for everyone. These rations are more than enough for a family. Discarded bread and rotten food are left over. In the war, obtaining this kind of food from the trash was considered almost a miracle. The Jews who are here have no worries. There is so much food here in the immigrant homes, but it is impossible to eat everything, and all that remains is scattered around . . . large quantities of wasted food . . .

After I rest for a few days, I "go out to my brothers." I go out to my immigrant brothers, friends, and acquaintances to see what's going on and how people feel in our old-new home. I meet them at every step, my many acquaintances. We exchange greetings, "*Sholem Aleichem*," "*Nu*, how are you?," "How's it going?" But then, after the question is asked, the positive atmosphere vanishes. A cloud, like that of Rosh Chodesh Elul [the month of atonement] appears on

---

2   This refers to DTT, a disinfectant sprayed on immigrants from Middle Eastern and Eastern European countries—M. M.

their faces, and in the sad melody of *selichot* [supplication prayers]; they answer me, "Ah, we didn't need to come here . . . It would have been better to stay in Germany where one could make a living . . . They didn't need to stand in line to eat . . . There was a better life there than here." I turn and leave in disgust, without saying goodbye to my acquaintances. I meet a second, third, fourth person, but I hear the same sinful words from them. "We remember the fish" [a reference to the complaints of the Israelites in the desert], I hear with every step. The "flesh pot" that was cooked and greased in our blood and the blood of our people is still there. It makes my heart sad. This is the real cold shower I felt. I didn't want to speak with them anymore, and I didn't want to see any acquaintances. I couldn't hear this talk any longer . . .

I went to the dining hall to bring food for my family. I stood in a long line of many people. Around me, I heard everyone grumbling and gawking, like geese. One topic: dissatisfaction with having come here. If they could have, my fellow immigrants would have returned to Europe, just like the Israelites said in the desert—"let us head back to Egypt." It boiled my blood. In bitter anger, I yelled, "What wicked people you are! The reincarnations of Dathan and Aviram and the spies [who scouted out the land of Israel] have entered you." What has happened to you that you are speaking with such bitterness about the land where every bit has been acquired through blood and where so many boys and girls have sacrificed themselves just for our sake and for our future!" None of the immigrants are hungry, God forbid, and no one is wandering around outside in the rain—what gives them the right to such despair and such talk? Everyone at the table sounds like the biblical Israelites in the desert who refused to accept the redemption the Creator of the World led them to. This, in truth, is the immigrant absorption process. It truly is hard going. People sit for five or six months in the immigration camp. Some sit there for eight months. But after everything, sitting in the camp is not, God forbid, endangering anyone's life, as I described before, and the question of food doesn't even occur to anyone. Almost 80% of those from our camp work and earn two Palestinian pounds a day, and even if life here wasn't so sweet in the beginning and we had to suffer a bit, is it really necessary to start with talk of "we remember the fish"? Where is our love of Zion? How has the focus changed from love of the land to politics?

During the year of the founding of the State of Israel, 230,000 Jews came to Israel. In the *camp*, there are now 60,000 Jews. This means that 170,000 Jews are already living in their homes, in normal living conditions living an Israeli life. Things are moving and progressing forward. The building of homes for immigrants—one can see it in every corner of the land. This aliyah costs millions—moving Jews from all corners of the earth in ships, airplanes, cars, and

trains to bring immigrants home. What sort of devil and evil spirit is roaming here among us, poisoning us? Could it be the same evil spirit that pursued Jewish fate for 2,000 years? Do they want to return to Munich, to Stuttgart, where the smoke is still rising from crematorium chimneys. Where? We were in every corner of the world. All of Europe is a cemetery where it is possible to continue the life of "Kasrilevka,"[3] which drowned in a sea of blood . . .
(Written by my grandfather, Yechiel Mikhael Becher, three weeks after he arrived in Israel in 1949. Translated from Yiddish by Yael Levi)

A Difficult Redemption—Mikhael's Integration into Israel

During his first months in Israel, my grandfather was harsh in his critiques of other immigrants who complained about the state's flaws. He saw them as ungrateful and petty—people who didn't understand the context of the events they were lucky to take part in. He insisted upon seeing the State of Israel as the realization of both his worldly and religious hopes. But with time, life in Israel tired even him.

After some time in an immigrant camp next to Ra'anana, my grandfather, grandmother, mother, and her siblings moved to a public housing project in Bat Yam. There, Jewish immigrants from around the world, Holocaust survivors from Europe, Polish Hassids, Egyptian bourgeois, Orthodox Lithuanians, traditional Yemenites, and refugees from Europe who traveled through Japan and South America on their way to Israel were brought together in a disorderly amalgam. These different groups were brought together in crowded buildings and became neighbors. Some came by choice, while others were brought without being asked. Of course, each family brought its own culture and spiritual world, but, despite their differences, they saw the new State of Israel as the realization of their aspirations and the dream of many generations of Jews.

The religious Jews from Eastern Europe banded together in an attempt to preserve the communities they had lost. Although Rabbi Miller was Lithuanian and my grandfather practiced Hasidic customs, they shared a common religious language. There were moments of friction between them: "I like Kant on his own and a sermon on its own," my grandfather would grumble when Rabbi Miller would mix philosophical anecdotes into his sermons. The Eastern European synagogue was located on one side of the street, and a house that served as the

---

3   A fictional shtetel from the stories of the writer Sholem Aleichem.

Middle Eastern synagogue was located on the other side. The women's section was in the back of my grandfather's synagogue, but, as a child, my mother would go with him and sit in the men's section. Savta Matel would stay at home, as was the custom of women in their family. My grandfather would rise at five thirty to pray exactly as the sun rose and learn Torah. In Israel, his daily routine returned to the way it had been before the Holocaust.

The young, new State of Israel had its own music to offer, but my grandfather preferred to listen to grand cantors who set biblical verses to music. He would listen to all of the greats—Koussevitzky, the Malavsky family (which also included women who sang), and Zevulun Kwartin. He would become the most emotional when hearing Kwartin's rendition of "Rabbi Yishmael purified himself," the famous liturgical poem about ten rabbis martyred by the Romans in the period after the destruction of the Second Temple.

Even in Israel, with all of its talk of redemption, it was still necessary to make a living. My grandparents didn't have a "red card"—the membership card of the Histadrut, Israel's national union—which was often needed in order to obtain a job. They saw joining the explicitly secular Mapai party and its union as a declaration of rebellion against God. The Zionism of Ben-Gurion and his ilk turned its back on the past and on tradition—an orientation that my grandparents were unwilling to accept.

Instead, my grandmother got a job delivering milk jugs and recruited my grandfather to the task. They would get up together in the early morning to complete the deliveries. The work was hard, and my grandmother sank into depression. After a few years, Rabbi Miller arranged work for my grandfather as a bank clerk, a job he held until he retired. He never forgot Rabbi Miller's kindness in helping him. Later, my grandmother became the housekeeper of a senior public servant in Agudat Yisrael, one of Israel's ultra-Orthodox parties.

My grandparents were scrupulous in their observance of religious commandments. They sent their children to religious schools—my mother went to Beis Yaakov, an ultra-Orthodox school. Her friends in the housing project came from different countries and cultures—a result of "the ingathering of the exiles"—and weren't always to my grandparents' liking. In particular, they disliked the family of her Egyptian friend. They had a bourgeois Jewish background and sought out a school that would be of equal quality to the schools they had left in Egypt. So they sent their daughter to a Christian, French-speaking school in Jaffa. My grandparents, for their part, feared that my mother would be snatched up by Christian priests; it was one fear, among other fears and anxieties, that they brought with them to Israel from Europe. In imaginary scenes that they relayed to my mother, priests lay in wait for them at every turn, intending to grab my mother and convert her to Christianity. Their worry had no basis in Israeli actuality, but, for them, it was real and tangible, in a genuinely physical manner—just like the fear of Holocaust survivors who would wander the neighborhood at night, waking the neighbors with their screams.

One time, my mother was going home at dusk and saw a priest on the other side of the street. She froze in place for several long minutes before realizing that the "priest" she feared was, in fact, the reflection of a triangular road hazard sign. She had inherited her parents' anxieties without once laying her eyes upon a Polish priest. Even the Land of Redemption might still be home to cruel and aggressive enemies for my grandparents. When my grandmother would happen upon a particularly large potato, she would happily declare that one could kill a gentile with such a thing, and when she passed a church or Christian cross, she would curse in Yiddish.

Matel tried to make their home similar to the one in Poland, and she worked hard at cultivating a garden outside the building. She had a generally positive outlook, happier than my grandfather's. She would sing, read newspapers, and listen to the radio. Despite their poverty, the meals were always abundant, with an appetizer and main course. Like my grandfather, my grandmother did not abandon her traditions. Before lighting Shabbat candles, she would say Yiddish *tekhines*, personal devotional prayers of supplication, and cry. These prayers, written in Eastern Europe and including individual requests, have also been forgotten in Israel. When my mother asked my grandmother why she was crying, she would answer that she was alone, dried-up wood, like a solitary stick.

My grandparents eventually left Bat Yam. The communal life of the new world didn't compare to that of the old world, nor did it offer redemption. They never found a new language, remaining suspended between worlds. They moved to the ultra-Orthodox city of Bnei Brak, where they lived until the end of their lives. My grandmother would read the Yiddish *Letzte Nayes* (Latest News), though my grandfather thought the newspaper was too worldly, too secular.

My grandfather disengaged from politics. He still voted for the ultra-Orthodox Poalei Agudat Yisrael party, and there were members of the Knesset who angered him; but those were battles from his former life that he had dragged to Israel. For example, he hated Yitzhak Gruenbaum, a leftist social-ist parliament member, who was an activist in Poland before the war and tried to ban religious representatives from the Polish Parliament. Over time, Israel's landscape ceased to interest him. He didn't walk among the hills dreaming of his biblical ancestors. Instead, every year, he would ascend Mount Zion to say kaddish in the Chamber of the Holocaust, located on the summit. Unlike Yad

Vashem, the Chamber of the Holocaust did not emphasize Zionism or redemption after the destruction.

In 1967, after the Israeli army conquered the Jewish holy sites in Jerusalem and the West Bank, my grandfather participated in an organized tour of the Western Wall in Jerusalem and the Tomb of the Patriarchs in Hebron. There remains a photo souvenir from his visit to the Kotel. He wrote on the picture: "in the pouring forth of my prayers before the Creator." In the photo, you can see him standing with an open prayer book, but there is no smile or look of spiritual connection on his face. This was a one-time tour. The following year, he returned to the memorial for the annihilated communities of Europe on Mount Zion.

My grandfather's traditional world didn't die, but it retreated into itself. Jewish national independence stunned traditionalism. Unable to contend with a new Jewish identity, my grandfather distanced himself from this new arena, from contemporary Judaism, and new politics. His disappointment in redemption's realization also came with his abandonment of new Jewish communal life.

Hear O Israel; the Kotel Is Our Kotel, the Kotel Is One

Unlike my grandfather, I prayed at the Western Wall for the entirety of my childhood. My family lived in the Old City's Jewish Quarter, and the Kotel was my first synagogue. At the beginning of the First Intifada, when I was not yet ten, we left the Jewish Quarter. My first political memory is of Palestinian protestors on the Temple Mount on Fridays, especially the smell of tear gas floating above the Western Wall and into our living room windows. The Kotel became a symbol of Israeli sovereignty and the struggle between Israel and the Palestinians, and not only a symbol of yearning for the Temple.

While traditional Judaism was unsuccessful in adapting to the existence of "the sovereign Jews," secular Judaism solidified, granting the new independent reality a nontraditional interpretation. Time after again, secular Judaism returned to the world of religious meaning and its ancient symbols of redemption. My grandfather avoided the Western Wall and looked inwards to his tradition. Simultaneously, Ben-Gurion's associates, who ostensibly favored rebellion against the old religious symbols, preserved the messianic redemptive status of the Kotel.

Jews have prayed at the Kotel for hundreds of years, long before the advent of the Zionist movement. But today, it's hard to imagine the pre-state Kotel. The last remnant of the Temple were a small area where Jewish men and women crowded together and cried over the exile of God's presence. This symbol of exile was notably in Jerusalem, in the Land of Israel. The Mughrabi Quarter, located behind the Kotel's prayer area, was also hundreds of years old—Salah a-Din's son built it in 1193. The relationship between the neighborhood's residents and the Jews who prayed at the Kotel was often rife with tension, and Jews were subject to regular harassment.

At the end of the nineteenth century, Baron Rothschild visited the Kotel and wanted to buy the site, yet the rabbinic sages of Jerusalem opposed the purchase. The author and poet Itamar Ben Avi, a secular Zionist and the son of Eliezer Ben Yehuda, who is credited as one of the creators of modern spoken Hebrew, announced that the neighborhood ought to be destroyed and a prayer plaza erected in its place. He called his book *Hear O Israel; the Kotel is our Kotel, the Kotel is One.*[4] He argued in favor of the unity of the people and sovereignty over the land, and, as his title makes clear, he swapped out God for the wall of the Temple.

The Israeli army conquered the Kotel in 1967, the moment that represented the victory of the Six-Day War. In one of the most iconic photos of the war, paratroopers look up longingly towards the Kotel; in another photo, Chief Military Rabbi Goren is seen blowing a shofar next to it. One day after conquering the Kotel, Ben-Gurion, who no longer held an official position, visited the site, together with Yaakov Yanai (the director of the National Parks Authority), Shimon Peres, Ezer Weizman (the then head of the Operations Directorate), and Teddy Kollek (the mayor of Jerusalem).[5] Ben-Gurion was irritated by its look: "The area needs to be cleaned up; the Kotel needs a better appearance." Teddy Kollek took responsibility for the task, and decided to destroy the Mughrabi Quarter. However, the Israeli army didn't want to participate in the demolition. Government officials were not directly involved in the destruction of the Mughrabi Quarter, despite giving the order to carry it out. The Organization of Contractors and Builders in Jerusalem, an independent group of civilians, was called to do this national work. Although some of the team were secular, it was carried out as though a religious ritual.

Eitan Ben Moshe, an engineering officer who found the contractors, described it as follows: "Taking into consideration the sanctity of Shabbat, with the conclusion of Shabbat, I received the directive to begin the

---

4   Itamar Ben Avi, *Shma Yisra'el, ha-kotel kotleinu ha-kotel ehad* (Jerusalem: Ha-Solel, 1928).
5   The description of the event is taken from two sources: Shmuel Bahat, "Why Was the Moghrabi Quarter Destroyed," *Judea and Samaria Research Studies* 24 (2017): 121–138 and Shmuel Bahat, "The Neighborhood before Our Wall: The Destruction of the Moghrabi Quarter near the Western Wall," *Et-mol* 250 (2018): 1–4.

evacuation of the plaza in the presence of the mayor, his deputies, the city's engineer, and a group of contractors. Mr. Z. Prosek received the honor of making havdalah[6] and those present could not hide their excitement, and tears of joy wet their faces. After this, the hammers started to strike amidst song and spiritual upliftment."

Residents of the neighborhood were offered compensation of two hundred Jordanian dinars, which some refused to accept, and they were given two hours to prepare for being expelled from their homes. Sadly, a Palestinian woman was killed inside her house during the demolition, while other people were saved only at the last minute. As a result, everyone from the neighborhood became refugees—between six hundred and fifteen hundred people. Today, some of their descendants live in the Shuafat refugee camp, while some fled to Jordan.

After destroying the buildings, the contractors declared themselves the Order of the Kotel and continued to meet for dozens of years to come. In a commemorative album released by the members of the order a year after event, there is a drawing by the artist Lea Majaro Mintz in which Jews are returning the Temple vessels to the Kotel—a sort of artistic response to the image on the Arch of Titus. The verse that the artist chose to incorporate in the work is taken from Isaiah's prophecy about God's revenge at the end of days: "The day of God is coming, of overflowing fury and wrath, to make the earth desolate, and to wipe out sinners upon it" (Isaiah 13:9). The name of the album, like the title of Itamar Ben Avi's book, is *Hear O Israel: the Kotel is our Kotel, the Kotel is One.*

In the days after the neighborhood was demolished, many in Israel complained about the operation; it had taken place under cover of darkness, without public discussion, and as an seemingly private initiative. There were also architectural concerns about the work—expanding the prayer plaza had ruined the character of the place. While in the past, the narrow alleyways of the Mughrabi Quarter led to the Kotel, which was revealed in all of its glory only in the final moment, a symbol of the future redemption that would occur in a single moment, now, the congregation area stood at the center. The Kotel became a footnote, a decorative ornament to a people that celebrated itself. Teddy Kollek, in an interview with Kol Yisrael, didn't deny these accusations:

> This was the biggest thing that we could do. And it's good that we did so immediately [. . .]. The place had a Diasporic atmosphere to it, a place for crying. There may have been a reason for this in the past. But this is not what we want for the

---

6   The ceremony that moves the Sabbath to a weekday—M. M.

future [. . .]. One day we will excavate the Kotel, restore it to how it was in the past, and see it stand in its glory as it was when it was part of the Jerusalem Temple. This will be suitable for the future of a united Jerusalem.

The Kotel remained a place of prayer, but not long after the construction the plaza, it also became a military symbol. Soldiers swore their allegiance to the Israeli army its base, holding a gun in one hand with a second hand placed atop a Tanakh. The loyalty of civilian soldiers to our military was, and still is, saturated with religious symbolism.

The destruction of the Mughrabi Quarter and the establishment of the Kotel Plaza as a holy site for the secular Jewish State are examples of the development of secular Zionism's religious characteristics in Israel. While traditional Judaism responded to Jewish sovereignty with political retreat and a turn inwards, the secular Judaism of independence adopted religious symbols and mixed the state and religion together.

Literary critic Baruch Kurzweil, one of the first people to fully understand secular Zionism's religious, messianic, and dangerous features, wrote in 1970:

Zionism and its daughter, the State of Israel, who arrived at the Western Wall using military conquest to realize national messianism, will never be able to forfeit the Wall and leave occupied parts of the Land of Israel without denying the very essence of their historiosophical conception of Judaism. Zionism as a form of actualization was caught in a net of its achievements. Abandoning them meant acknowledging its failures as the voice and implementor of Judaism's historical continuity. The secular Messiah cannot retreat: he can only die. With this, he pays the price of his presumptuous attempt to give over the fate of Judaism to the secular cycle of history. Zionism as a form of actualization should have been clear from its beginnings that discourse and achievement are most intimate with death. Retreating reveals a break in the historical continuum—which it and only it is the truth. Everything else is an illusion. It is impossible to stop the fast movements of messianic apocalypse to allow passengers to disembark and look at the spectacular views of the Day of God.[7]

---

7 Baruch Kurzweil, *Le-Nokhaḥ ha-mevukhah ha-ruḥanit shel yemeinu* (Ramat Gan: Yad Kurzweil, Bar-Ilan University, 1976), 195.

Precisely because he was religious, Kurzweil was able to identify the spiritual features of secular Zionism, especially regarding the Kotel. Religious Zionism fits itself into secular, messianic discourse, and discussion on the religious and national place of the Kotel continues to raise controversy in Israeli society. Rabbi Shlomo Aviner, one of the most prominent spokespeople of Religious Zionism, recently wrote an article on the sanctity of the Kotel in the religious magazine *Srugim*:

> The Israeli military has great sites for holding rituals, but many commanders want them to occur specifically at the Kotel, a small, modest, suitable, Jewish, pure, and holy place. Because indeed, every Jew is holy inside. Of course, in reality, there are still complications, but within the soul, it stands a holy nation, a pure nation, a believing nation. And the matter has been revealed at the Kotel, where everyone, of all practices and opinions, agreed to behave with purity and holiness at the same holy site which stands in front of our holy Temple.[8]

Rabbi Aviner points to the religious emotion latent within Israeli secularism, and I think he is correct. I am not sure that the values of Religious Zionism, represented in this case by Rabbi Aviner, contradict the values of secular Zionism, as is often thought to be the case. Teddy Kollek, Ben-Gurion's emissary, decided to confiscate the property of the Mughrabi Quarter residents to establish a site of religious worship, and those who demolished the neighborhood acted out of religious feeling and religious passion.

To understand how close Rabbi Aviner's religious feelings are to those of the destroyers of the Mughrabi Quarter, it is enough to look at the title of his essay quoted above: "Hear O Israel: The Kotel is Our Kotel, the Kotel is One."

Jewish Values Versus the State's Ethics: The Case of Qibya

The case of construction of the Kotel Plaza is one instance of religion having to grapple with Jewish sovereignty. But it was not the first time that religious leaders needed to wrestle with the issue of the State of Israel's use of force. Questions

---

8   Shlomo Aviner, "שמע ישראל, הכותל כותלינו, הכותל אחד," *Srugim*, February 1, 2016, https://www.srugim.co.il/137997-שמע-ישראל-הכותל-כותלינו-הכותל-אחד.

about the use of force, on the one hand, versus Jewish values and sovereignty, on the other, were raised in the very first years following the foundation of the state.

On October 14, 1953, soldiers from Unit 101, as part of a joint operation with the Paratroopers Brigade, killed more than sixty residents of the village of Qibya, primarily women and children, in an attack meant to avenge the murder of a mother and her two children in the Jewish town of Yehud. The operation's bloody outcome led to a conversation on the meaning of Jewish political power. Among the respondents was Professor Yeshayahu Leibowitz. He was one of the lone Jewish voices to challenge the state's use of force and its use of God to justify violent action.

When I was around thirteen, my father bought my older sister Leibowitz's collection of essays *Judaism, the Jewish People, and the State of Israel*.[9] I took the book and searched out the political chapters. Leibowitz's opinions were always incisive and stated with complete self-confidence. Unlike other thinkers, he never considered hiding his views, even when they were unpopular. Leibowitz was among the first to write about the ethical corruption entailed in ruling over millions of Palestinians, and his work aroused many people's anger. For me, Leibovitch had particular importance—he was a religious Jew opposed to the occupation. He was my spokesperson.

The collection features his writing on the occupation, but for me, the most important essay is one from 1953, "After Qibya." Few people in Israel opposed the massacre at the time and even fewer opposed it for ethical and religious reasons. Leibowitz published his short yet harsh essay in the Mapai journal *B'Terem*, and many read, and still remember, his position. Dozens of years later, the paper continues to influence and mold many people's political thinking, including my own. However, despite this influence in recent years, I doubt some of Leibowitz's unequivocal declarations.

1. Leibowitz: There Are No Jewish Political Values

The editors of the *B'Terem* publication described the massacre in the introduction to Leibowitz's essay as follows:

> On October 13, 1953, Arab infiltrators from the area of Qibya—
> an Arab village in Samaria—threw a grenade into a Jewish home
> in the immigration settlement of Yehud. As a result, a mother
> and her two children were killed in their sleep. This act, which

---

9   Yeshayahu Leibowitz, "After Qibya," in *Ha-Yahadut, ha-'am ha-yehudi, u-medinat Yisrael*, (Jerusalem: Schoken, 1975), 229–234.

followed a continuous series of murder attacks in the area, led to a revenge attack by the Israeli army. Israeli forces attacked Qibya, which is located a considerable distance beyond the ceasefire line, on October 14. Over 50 residents were killed during the operation, and four homes were destroyed. The attack led to an international uproar. Israel's public campaign to explain this operation—that it was carried out against a backdrop of bitter anger within Israel because of the crimes of the infiltrators from the same area—was not accepted by the international community and the UN Security Council severely rebuked Israel.[10]

Leibowitz came out against the operation with sharp and outspoken criticism.[11] In his opinion, even if it were possible to provide security justifications for the Qibya massacre, the act itself was "cursed" and was ethically untenable.[12] Leibowitz's central question was how the Israeli army might have acted in such a cursed way. In the final section of the essay, which is also the most often quoted, he presents a possible explanation for the soldiers' behavior.[13] This essay also helps to elucidate his position on the relationship between religious and political life. Leibowitz distinguishes between ethics and politics, on the one hand, and religiosity and Judaism, on the other, and cautions against explaining "Judaism" through political and ethical lenses. The Qibya massacre, as far as he is concerned, exemplifies the danger of mixing these domains and granting ethical-religious meaning to sovereignty:

> There is, however, a specifically Jewish side in the case of Qibya, but this is not an ethical problem but a pronounced religious problem. We must ask ourselves: where do these youth come from, who feel no restraint or spiritual hindrance in carrying out

10 Ibid., 229.

11 Despite Leibowitz's unequivocal claims, as years went by some scholars questioned the accuracy and clarity of his claims. See Zev Harvey, "After Qibya: Yeshayahu Leibowitz, Leon Roth, and Nehama Leibowitz," in Yeshayahu Leibowitz: Bein shamranut le-radikaliut, ed. Aviezer Ravitzky (Jerusalem: Van Leer Institute, 2007), 354–365.

12 Leibowitz's argument that the massacre at Qibya was "cursed" yet justified is problematic for many reasons. See Yehuda Melzer, "On the Curse," in The Book of Yeshayahu Leibovitz, ed. Asa Kasher and Yaakov Levinger (Tel Aviv: University of Tel Aviv, 1997), 128–136.

13 Interestingly, this section was not part of the original article printed in BeTerem and originally appeared as part of Leibovitch's response to a question on the article. It was only later added to the article itself.

this horror with their own hands when the internal or external urge for a revenge attack is present? And indeed, these youths were not the rabble but rather the youths who grew up and were educated on the values of Zionist education, with the importance given to other people and society. This matter is the result of the use of the religious category of holiness for issues and values that are social, national, and political, which is used prevalently among us in youth education and public conversation: concepts of holiness—that means, the fundamental concepts beyond which all notions of human thought and evaluation are transferred to the mundane, whereas all of a person's values and all obligations and roles that spring from them are mundane and not absolutely meaningful. Homeland, State, nation—these are lofty obligations and positions, which sometimes require even challenging actions, yet they will never be made holy. They will constantly be tested and subject to criticism of something above them. A person can act without any restraint on religious matters, perhaps only on these matters. We uproot holiness's categories and transfer them onto cases for which they were not intended, with all the danger bound up in such a distorted use. This original sin of our education is already reflected in our Declaration of Independence—the phrase "Rock of Israel," which appears at the end of the text as a collision between two public camps, collusion that adds no honor to either camp: the secular people and State, who removed the meaning from this phrase, offered the term as a bribe to the religious minority, which did not avoid accepting it, even though they knew the two-facedness latent in the use of this holy term. The term "Rock of Israel" of King David, Isaiah the Prophet, and in the blessing after the Shema during Shacharit [morning prayers]—is not in Israel but beyond Israel and all values, the causes and human revelations, personal and collective together. "Rock of Israel" in the Declaration of Independence is in Israel itself—it is the identity and human strength of Israel: Israel as revealed in history. However, the use of this phrase from the Bible and siddur for our human feelings and consciousness and the driving forces of our religious-national actions—this use causes even situations of holiness—that means of absolute validity—that are bound up in this term are passed on to these values. If the nation and its welfare and the homeland and its security are holy, and if the sword itself is the "Rock of Israel," then also Qibya is possible and permissible.[14]

Leibowitz argued that the Qibya massacre was "the result of the use of religious categories of holiness for matters and values that are social, national, and political, which are used prevalently among us in youth education and public discourse."[15] The state's use of religious concepts is religiously invalid and necessarily leads to the ill-advised and unchecked use of military force. The problem lies in applying the religious idea of "the Rock of Israel" (a phrase used in the Israeli declaration of independence) to the State of Israel and in describing the state with holy concepts of absolute validity. If the state and its power is sacred, it cannot be restrained. Religiosity, when it is used to validate sovereignty, also validates throwing restraint to the wind. I, too, share this concern.

However, Leibowitz's argument is not only about how state action is justified through religious terminology—it is much broader. According to his view here, the Torah neither tries nor cares to determine political or ethical behavior. As we have seen, Leibowitz saw the Qibya massacre as morally invalid, even if it was possible to justify it by other means. There are specific actions that are categorically invalid, even if some defense of them can be found. Leibowitz offered proof for his argument from Jacob's response to Simeon and Levi's actions against the people of Shechem. Even though the act could have been considered justified because Shechem "defiled their sister," it is still ethically invalid, and, because of this, Jacob cursed them.

> It is indeed possible to account and give ground for, to explain and justify, the actions of Shechem-Qibya from the perspective of all ethical principles that can be considered and calculated rationally. However, an ethical postulate is not within the framework of consideration and calculation, which springs a curse on all of these just and correct considerations and calculations. The act of Shechem and our father Jacob's curse, at the time which he showed his sons the end of days—is an example of the troubling

---

14 Leibovitch, *After Qibya*, 230.
15 Ibid.

ethical problem that there may be an action that is accounted for and reasoned, and even justified—and even so, it is cursed.[16]

To ensure that the reader does not conclude that the Qibya massacre was specifically "Jewishly" invalid, Leibowitz unequivocally writes that there are no "Jewish ethics":

> "Jewish ethics' is one of the most dubious concepts—and not only because ethics cannot tolerate adjectives which diminish them and cannot be "Jewish" or "not Jewish": the very category of "Jewish ethics" is an inherent contradiction for anyone who does not intentionally ignore the religious content and meaning of Judaism—meaning, anyone who does not falsify Judaism.[17]

An ethical system does not deal with the connection between a person and God but rather with how people treat one another, and it is thus not a religious system. Leibowitz opposed the idea that the Jewish tradition has obligatory political content. God does not care about our political worldviews; He only cares that we carry out religious commandments. The performance of commandments and ethical-political behavior are worlds apart.

How, then, does Leibowitz explain the development of a Jewish ethical outlook? He claims that such an outlook developed from historical circumstances but has no connection to the "essence" of Judaism itself. He writes at the beginning of his essay:

> In terms of ethics and conscience, we have lived for generations in an artificial incubator, in which we could grow and cultivate values and content that were not put to the test of reality. We saw ourselves, and to some extent were seen by others, as overcoming one of the most terrible inclinations which ambush the human soul and the feeling of disgust for the frequent revelation of atrocities in human society: the inclination for intergroup bloodshed. In our self-pride about this, we have ignored—or we have tried to ignore—the fact that in our historical situation, this sort of bloodshed was not one of the means our group could have used to protect its existence or satisfy its needs and desires.

---

16 Melzer, "On The Curse."
17 Leibovitch, *After Qibya*, 230.

In other words, Jewish skepticism towards violence was the expression of a people who had not tested the use of force and therefore could pride themselves on mercy, patience, compassion, and more.

I find this position difficult. The sharp contrast Leibowitz demands—between religious texts and the historical contexts they were written in—never existed and never can exist. While it is true that Jews wrote in shifting political contexts, it is impossible to understand texts outside of the political context in which they were written. But this does not mean that these texts have no meaning for us, nor does it mean that Judaism is apathetic to ethical values.

How ought people to act within their families and within their communities? How should a good Jew behave? Why are some actions blessed while other actions are cursed? Answers to these questions are anything but rare in Jewish sources; indeed, they are the essence of Jewish sources. Leibowitz, however, seemingly requires religious people to alienate themselves from the generations-long tradition of ethical content found in these answers.

It is also worth noting that, despite Leibowitz's claim to the contrary, not all Jewish texts express the "feeling of disgust for the frequent revelation of atrocities in human society." Alongside values of mercy, patience, and overcoming the inclination to kill, Jewish tradition also includes texts that express fear, hatred towards gentiles, and supremacy over gentiles. It contains texts on wars, including obligatory religious wars.[18]

We must grapple with both of these sides of the tradition. The fact that a given text was written in particular historical and social circumstances certainly does not make it irrelevant. Still, it does require us to understand the text in its context and choose a suitable interpretive path in light of it. As a person with freedom and power, I can engage with texts that demonstrate trepidation and revulsion towards gentiles, written from a place of weakness and fear. Rather than pretending they don't exist, I prefer to read these texts critically and compassionately. But at the same time, and unlike Leibowitz, I both can, and want to, see the strength within Jewish texts on compassion, patience, and mercy, even though they were written by people who lacked power. Doing so is necessary for my moral education as a believing Jew.

I cannot, nor do I want to, distance myself from the ethical content of these texts. I cannot, nor do I want to, pray to God at synagogue or speak about God with compassion, awe, and love (and yes, also about God who exacts revenge), while at the same time ignoring the implication of these words in my civic, political life. Leibowitz requires the religious person to live a divided, compartmen-

---

18 Chapter five in this book analyzes at length the category of obligatory religious wars.

talized life, a life that is split into two estranged worlds. Yet the requirement for ethical behavior is part of my religious world; it is anchored in the famous statement of the midrash in the Sifre (Ekev 11:22): "Just as the Holy-Blessed-One is called merciful, so too should you be merciful."

Moreover, abandoning religious-ethical language does not make such discourse disappear; instead, it allows others in Israel to take control of the Jewish language and use it for their purposes. Leibowitz's position, which requires people to limit their religious lives to their relationship with God and sever religion from their ties to their communities and surroundings, left religious ethics in the hands of other interpreters.

2.   Rabbi Shaul Yisraeli and the Creation of the War of Vengeance

Leibowitz's essay was not the only religious response to the Qibya massacre. Rabbi Shaul Yisraeli, one of Religious Zionism's leading thinkers at the time, also took on the case and wrote a detailed legal responsum explaining why the operation in Qibya was not only religiously permissible but was, in fact, obligatory.

The writing and thought of Religious Zionist rabbis are rife with the attempt to resolve the Torah's core principles with the reality of state violence. After the Qibya massacre and other cases, Religious Zionist rabbis consistently and publicly offered justifications for every action without being asked to do so.

Rabbi Yisraeli was one of the most important legal decidors of Religious Zionism; among other roles, he served as the rosh yeshiva (head of seminary) of Mercaz HaRav, which later became the flagship institution of Religious Zionism. His responsa on issues related to the use of force are collected in his book *Amud HaYemini*. After Qibya, he wrote a long responsum exploring revenge attacks from different perspectives.

In the fifth section of his extensive responsum, Yisraeli discusses the issue of killing innocent people, especially children, as part of revenge attacks carried out by the State of Israel:

> However, it is a commandment from the law of revenge. This is learned from what the Torah commands about revenge in the Midian War (Numbers 31). This is the term of Maimonides, "delivering Israel from an enemy," meaning, based on the verse, "Attack the Midianites and defeat them for they attacked you." And Maimonides considered this part of the Torah, on the verse "Moses became angry," which is brought in the Sifre that Pinchas said to him, "As you have commanded, we have done." And

Nachmanides explained that Pinchas thought this was according to the laws of a regular war, which requires that women and children be left alive. And Moses explained to him that this is a war of vengeance, in which children must also be killed because of revenge . . .

If so, we have learned from here that there is a particular concept of a war of revenge, and this is a war against those who attack Israel, and such a war has specific regulations. And in any case, the commandment certainly exists in perpetuity, just as it did for Midian, because we learn from Midian according to the principle of *binyan av* [in which something derived from a particular verse is applied to all other similar cases].

And according to this, it seems that regarding what was written that in a case where they [enemies] have not come [to fight] but are only preparing to come, it is not considered an obligatory religious war—this applies only in a case where they have never come [to fight]. But if they came earlier and then retreated but their goal was to return, they are considered attackers of Israel. So then, according to all opinions, the laws of a war of vengeance can be applied to them, which is a religious obligation. All the rules of war apply, and there is no obligation to be precise in carrying out the operation to cause harm only to those who took part in it, for this is the nature of war, that the righteous perish alongside the wicked [. . .]. The conclusion of all of this is that there is a place for revenge operations against those who attack Israel, and such activity falls under the category of an obligatory religious war. And any tragedy or harm that comes upon the rioters, their allies, or their children, they are the ones who are responsible for it, and they shall bear that iniquity. And there is no obligation to abstain from revenge operations out of a concern that innocent people will be harmed, for we are not the instigators, but instead, they are, and we are blameless.

Indeed, intending to harm children *ab initio* has no grounding except regarding the sin of idolatry. Because of this, it is advisable to keep oneself from touching them. And the God of goodness will see the people's distress and will attack its attackers and uproot them from the land of the living. And through us, the verse will be fulfilled: "No weapon formed against you shall succeed, and you shall defeat any tongue that contends with you at law; such is the inheritance of servants of God, and their righteousness is through me, declares God." [19]

For those who are familiar with responsa literature, Rabbi Yisraeli's legal moves indeed appear very strange. Usually, in responsa literature, halakhic decisors describe an interpretive chain that begins with the rabbinic sages of the Talmud and continues to other halakhic decisors. The authors see themselves as continuing one of the existing interpretive strands. Rabbi Yisraeli, however, knowing that the Jewish interpretive tradition opposes violent revenge, does not do this. He himself surveyed the sources and demonstrated for many pages that Jewish authorities unequivocally prohibit killing children and any act of killing that is not for self-defense. To justify the revenge attack carried out by the combatants of Unit 101, which included the killing of women and children, Rabbi Yisraeli created a new and dubious interpretive strand. He turns to the Bible and uses the story of the Children of Israel's revenge against the Midianites to derive an entirely new religious obligation. In his opinion, just as the Children of Israel were commanded to kill all of the Midianites as an act of revenge, so too does the state have the authority to kill groups of "aggressors" following the law of retribution, including women and children.

Rabbi Yisraeli's interpretive innovation relies upon a direct turn to the Bible and completely ignores the rabbinic interpretive tradition. He concludes from two aspects of the biblical story: the Midianites are "attackers," and the Israelites took revenge against them. He suggests that the law regarding the Midianites can be applied as the law for all "attackers." Indeed, he writes that this "commandment certainly exists in perpetuity." However, there is no traditional interpretation that claims that revenge must be taken against any attacker. The idea that the secular State of Israel can determine to whom the laws of "attackers" apply is certainly strange from a religious perspective. Rabbi Yisraeli's "certainty" regarding the commandment's perpetual legal force is his innovation. In the end, he created a new type of war: "a war of vengeance."

Rabbi Yisraeli's interpretation has no precedent in traditional halakha; the entire tradition pushes in the opposite direction, that is, towards the view that it is forbidden to kill innocent people for revenge. So why does he depart from rabbinic tradition and dismiss it as irrelevant? Because of his desire to justify the sovereign State of Israel and its military activities.

---

19 Shaul Yisraeli, 'Amud Ha-yemini, ch. 24, part 5, secs. 30–35 (Jerusalem: Eretz Hemda, 1992).

Following the Qibya massacre, Rabbi Yisraeli created ex nihilo, the concept of a commandment to exact revenge through war. By doing so, he established a new and horrifying tradition—one which goes against everything that has been written about capital law in halakha and contradicts the absolute position of the abundant sources that prohibit killing for revenge, and particularly the killing of children.

Rabbi Yisraeli's ruling is very difficult, but we must remember that his writing did not directly pave the path to the Qibya massacre, as he wrote his responsum only after the fact. His ruling is an outcome of the operation, not its reason. How, though, did the officers and participants in the operation think about it?

3. The Position of Ben-Gurion and the Those Who Carried Out the Shoshana Operation: "The patience of some people in the border settlements ran out."

Leibowitz and Rabbi Yisraeli have much in common. Both of them are observant Jews. Both of them are Zionists. Both of them responded to an operation executed without their prior knowledge and which had not taken their opinions into account. But what about those who planned and carried out the attack? Did they indeed act due to an education of state holiness, as Leibovitch claimed? Examining the justifications given by those directly responsible for the massacre reveals a more troubling view than the one Leibowitz and Yisraeli attributed to them. But first, we must examine what happened in Qibya on November 1953.

The massacre, or to use its official name, the Shoshana Operation, was a revenge attack in response to a murder in the Jewish town of Yehud. The action was the first joint activity between Unit 101, the Israeli military's commando unit, whose soldiers wore plain clothes and were headed at the time by Ariel Sharon, and the Paratroopers Brigade. The goal was to blow up buildings in the village of Qibya for deterrence. The morning after the operation, it came to light that the Israeli army had killed sixty-nine Palestinians, about two-thirds of whom were women and children.

To this day, we do not know everything that happened that night. However, we do know that the cabinet met without the serving foreign minister, Moshe Sharett, to plan the mission. According to a biography by Gabi Sheffer, Sharett, who was considered too dovish, was intentionally left out of the decision-making process.

Some of those who were involved in the massacre claim to this day that there was no intention to kill innocents, that they did not know people were still in the houses. Others, however, claim that avoiding causing harm was not the top priority of the field forces; and others still have said that the killing was intentional. Though not with one of the main military groups, one soldier described what happened:

> We came back from the operation. Yair Rosenfeld from Degania Bet slept in the room with me. His face was as gray as a sack. I asked, "What happened?" He told me that a ten-year-old boy stood on the main road when he entered the village. A living soul was not to be found in the village. They asked the boy where the villagers were staying. He said that they had gone to Budrus. We understood that the village was empty. Yair and one of the paratroopers entered a house that was ready for an explosion. A woman with two children sat on the floor. The paratrooper, who spoke Arabic, told her to leave. She was frightened, felt safe in her home, and refused to leave. All of their attempts to remove her were futile. The sappers shouted, "Detonate." They jumped outside, and the woman and two children were killed. Afterward, they said that our intelligence officer, Shlomo Gruber, heard the cry of a child inside a house after the sappers yelled "detonate." He hurried inside, endangering his own life, and rescued the child and himself at the last moment.[20]

There are several versions of the official order for the operation. One states that the goal was to "attack the village of Qibya, occupy it temporarily, and carry out the maximum destruction and harm to people, hoping to drive the village residents away from their homes [...]. Intrusion into the villages of Shuqba and Ni'lin, to destroy several homes and kill residents and soldiers in the village."[21] Other versions do not include the directive for maximum harm to people.

Whether the killing was carried out intentionally or unwittingly, those who executed the operation called it a success, even after they were made aware of its outcome. This is what the commander of Unit 101, Ariel Sharon, said two years after the event after his role in the paratroopers:

> Qibya fell. With it fell, at least for us, the myth of the unconquerable Arab village. When we returned from Qibya, we did

---

20 Uri Milstein, "Unit 101: What Exactly Happened at the Retribution Mission in Qibya?" [Hebrew], *Maariv*, October 14, 2016, https://www.maariv.co.il/news/military/Article-560232.

21 Ibid.

not return drunk with victory. Although outwardly, we felt that the Israeli army was on one side, and there was Unit 101 on the other. A unit that indeed numbers 25 people, without which the Israeli army would be unable to move further. This was a good feeling but not healthy. Whoever undertook self-examination saw that, in reality, only the operation in Qibya itself succeeded. The two operations in Ni'lin were not carried out following the directives. I assume that there were certainly those who blessed these failures the day after when the operation in Qibya came to light. We did some soul-searching and concluded that it was clearer to us in the field despite our knowledge of the enemy [. . .]. Our self-confidence increased greatly, but what was clear was that, in reality, only the big operation succeeded. When our investigation of the matter began, the necessity for independent officers, who can independently implement the tasks, became clear to us. This commanders' view continued to bother us for many months, even years after.[22]

From Sharon's reflection, one can see that he did not see a problem with killing innocent people, and it is possible that he even wanted such an outcome. The only problem with the operation was that those in charge had not internalized the necessity of a full-scale operation in Qibya and that the paratroopers did not act professionally or violently enough. It is important to note that he does not justify the action with terminology related to holiness but as part of an existential-security necessity. "We were not drunk with victory," he explained, but moral concerns did not bother him. The soul-searching that Sharon references is an operational soul-searching—how to carry out this type of mission more effectively next time.

There is a clear gap between how Sharon describes and justifies Qibya and Leibowitz and Yisraeli's viewpoint. According to Leibowitz, the massacre is the outcome of ascribing holiness to the state. But Sharon didn't need terminology related to holiness; he explained his actions and those of his soldiers with reference to national security interests. At least in his claims about "holiness," Leibowitz did not correctly diagnose the motivations and justifications of the soldiers and officers involved.

---

22 Taken from Ariel Sharon's parting words to his unit on April 15, 1957, quoted in Amir Oren, "Exhausted and Depressed: Ariel Sharon Exposed, Beaten, Sad and Placated," *Walla News*, April 26, 2019, https://news.walla.co.il/item/3232170.

This was the position of the top military leaders. But what was the opinion of the heads of state? Years after the event, when his thoughts no longer had political implications, Ben-Gurion claimed that the operation had been problematic because of its moral consequences. But at the time of the operation, Ben-Gurion thought that it was successful and even said to Sharon that "it doesn't matter what the nations of the world say; it matters how the Arabs of the area respond, and from that perspective, the incursion succeeded." His stance, like that of the military leaders, was utilitarian.

Six days after the massacre, following an intensive international investigation, Ben-Gurion understood that he could not entirely disavow it and put out a statement. He expressed sadness about the killing of innocent people. At the same time, however, he and the Israeli government sidestepped any responsibility and instead blamed the Jewish residents of the border areas, Mizrahim, and Holocaust survivors, for the bloodshed. He claimed that the residents of Israel's periphery towns had received weapons to protect themselves and used them for an unplanned revenge attack; but he knew that the "new Jews" in the army were responsible for what happened.

> The border settlements in Israel, largely Jewish refugees from Arab countries or the remnants of the Nazi concentration camps, have been the target for many years of these murderous attacks and have exercised great restraint. They justly demanded protection for their lives from their government—and the Israeli government distributed weapons to them and trained them to defend themselves. However, the armed forces beyond the Jordan did not stop their criminal attacks until some people's patience with the border settlements ran out. Then, after the murder of a mother and her two children in the village of Yehud, they attacked the village of Qibya beyond the border, which was one of the main centers of the murderous gangs [...]. The Government of Israel unequivocally rejects the foolish and fantastical version—as if 600 men from the Israeli army took part in an operation against the village of Qibya. We conducted a full investigation, and it is evident that not even the smallest military unit was absent from camp the night of the attack on Qibya.[23]

---

23 "Ben-Gurion: Nobody Is as Upset as Our Government if at Qibya Innocent Blood Was Spilt," *Herut*, October 20, 1953.

4.   Jacob Glatstein and the Death of Religious Judaism

While Leibowitz argued that the atrocities of Qibya sprung from the use of religious terminology in political discourse and that ethical behavior has no connection to religious obligations, other thinkers saw the Qibya massacre as a genuine betrayal of "Judaism." Jacob Glatstein is not well-known enough in the Israeli literary canon, but he was one of the most important Yiddish-language poets of the twentieth century. Born in Lublin in eastern Poland, he immigrated to the United States during World War I. In the world of Yiddish poetry, he is known as one of the founders of the inzikhist (introspectivist) movement. The poets in the movement rejected the symbolic and romantic poetry of the founding generation of Yiddish poetry in the United States. Instead, they sought out a personal and experiential perspective on the reality around them.

In 1953, Glatstein wrote a poem in Yiddish about the Qibya massacre. His interpretation opened a window for me onto the religious world that I knew from childhood. Moreover, he offered me new tools, which I had been unable to find in my Israeli-Jewish milieu, for reflecting on state power—both Jewish and critical lenses.

Qibya[24]

A

Anger, revenge, smoke.
A small camp with murder in their eyes.
Girded with bow and arrow,
In treachery of night,
My brothers
Annihilated the mercy within,
And defiled the parchment of my life.
My God of the patient study-house.
It is difficult to forgive such devilish bravery.

B

My People, my People of mercy,
My familiar Jew.
I won't give you up
For the greatest arsenals of bravery.
People of my *good* father,

---

24 Jacob Glatstein, "Qibya" [translated from the Yiddish by Adi Mahalel], *In Geveb*, February 21, 2016, https://ingeveb.org/texts-and-translations/qibya.

On foreign Polish soil.
How much did you train me in goodness,
From my cheder years onward.
My pride, my chosen one.
Exilic determination.
Do not liberate yourself from my righteous little corner.
Do not go away to life imprisonment,
With bloody chains on your hands.

C
My dear enemy, my strong hand
Will also be just.
The Yiddish word
Will not be desecrated.
The place where the peace stone
Will be laid,
Will be rock-solid and pure.
And when we count all the dead,
We will heal the mournful wounds,
With compassion, with faith;
That even on the battlefield,
In the shameful, dark night,
Our sons must be Jews of light,
Not murderous aggressors,
But defenders, victors, exalted.

Patience, claims Glatstein, is the organizing political value of the Jewish house of worship. Patience leads to mercy; patience leads to compassion; patience leads to spiritual upliftment and moving closer to God. The evil value, as opposed to patience, is the value of revenge. Unlike Rabbi Yisraeli, who viewed revenge as a value that characterizes Judaism in the age of sovereignty, Glatstein believed that the Judaism of the beit midrash, in its essence, is a patient Judaism. If revenge requires killing, patience requires mercy and compassion. I feel a strong connection to this world of values.

Yet, for Glatstein, it seems, a Judaism of patience is the consequence of lacking political power. The Jewish house of worship belongs on "foreign Polish soil," and all sovereignty is a move towards "life imprisonment." Although he fights against the Jewish Israeli ethics of power, patient Judaism is the Judaism of the past, in his opinion—a Judaism that can only exist when Jews do not have sovereignty. Maybe it will return in the future, but it is impossible in the present. It sometimes seems that traditional Judaism and its substantive, ethical language are, for Glatstein, in the process of extinction. In his sad poem "The Dead Will Not Praise God," he writes about Lublin, the city of his birth, located not far from my grandfather's village: "We received the Torah on Mount Sinai / and in Lublin, we gave it back. / The dead do not praise God. / The Torah was given for the living. / And as surely as we all stood together/ at the Law Giving, / So surely we all died in Lublin."[25] Unlike Leibowitz, Glatstein sees positive, ethical content in Judaism. But like Leibowitz, he believes that this content is dependent upon historical context, such that a Jew cannot be patient within sovereign Israel. The ethics that my grandfather and Glatstein held dear were murdered in Lublin, on foreign Polish soil.

5.   The Fifth Option: The Value of Patience in an Era of Israeli Sovereignty

The perspectives of those who responded to the Qibya massacre differed from one another: Glatstein and Leibowitz opposed the massacre for different reasons. At the same time, Sharon and Rabbi Yisraeli supported it for different reasons. Yet despite this, all of the opinions above rely upon one central assumption—Israeli sovereignty has transformed the Jews into a new people. All four positions examine "Jewish ethics" from the state's perspective rather than from that of the individual or the community. Some mourn the destruction of Diaspora Jewry, and some rejoice in it. Still, they all agree: Jewish patience and the ethics of traditional Judaism were relevant only in the Diaspora, and the Diaspora has ended. Those from the Religious Zionist camp propose that this redemption is religious. Those from the secular Zionist camp hold that the Jewish people were redeemed from Diasporic religion and now inhabit a secular Jewish existence. Even Glatstein sees the establishment of the State of Israel as a transition to a new kind of existence and argues that traditional Judaism has died.

But there is a fifth option: the existence of the State of Israel does not exempt Jews from their ethical obligations. The new reality of a state—a state in which Jews are the majority—does not make traditional Judaism irrelevant in the public sphere. Even seventy years later, the existence of the State of Israel does not nullify our ethical obligations or our Judaism. The State of Israel neither realizes redemption nor negates the need for redemption. The State of Israel is the political activity of some parts of the Jewish people. The question

---

25   Jacob Glatstein, "The Dead do Not Praise God," in *Anthologies*, vol. 1, *An Anthology of Modern Yiddish Literature*, ed. Joseph Leftwitch (Berlin: De Gruyter, 1974), 238

that interests me is not "How should a Jewish state act?," but "How should traditional Jews and traditional communities act when they have power and independence?" And here, by examining individual behavior, it is possible to see a different common denominator among the different positions described above. The thinkers discussed understood Qibya as an act of revenge. Rabbi Yisraeli spoke positively about wars of vengeance, while Glatstein's view was negative. Leibowitz chose an in-between position—a justified yet cursed act.

The value of patience is the counter-value, which stands in opposition to the value of revenge. That is what it seems from Glatstein's writing, who identifies the great enemy of revenge against Qibya as "the patient study-house." Ben-Gurion himself believed the same, claiming (falsely) that the Qibya operation was carried out by people whose "patience had run out." The option that I suggest is that the traditional Jew must behave with patience, including within the context of life in a sovereign state. If I want to live according to the value of patience, I must examine what this value means.

In Numbers 12:3, when Aaron and Miriam gossip about Moses's Kushite wife and his prophecy, Moses does not respond. It is immediately noted that "Moses himself was very humble, more so than any person on the face of the earth." Rashi interprets the word "humble" as "modest and patient." Patience means the decision to forego violent action from a place of humility. In this case, it is a value attributed to the prophet Moses, the person who was closest to God. This is the position of an individual with significant power who chooses to curb his power or refrain from exercising it. Eliezer Papo, a rabbi who lived in Bulgaria in the eighteenth century and wrote the virtue ethics book *Pele Yoetz*, also wrote about the value of patience:

> how good and how pleasant is the good value, necessary for all people, the great according to their greatness and the small according to their smallness; if he is the head of the people, he must be patient in enduring the burden of the people, and in patiently suffering the insults of evil people who oppose him and act towards them and treat them with pleasantness.[26]

My contention with Leibowitz is about the necessity and obligation to enlist the world of traditional Jewish values to create a political position regarding power. Leibowitz claimed that the term "Jewish ethics" is irrelevant because, among other reasons, "in terms of ethics and conscience, we have lived

---

26   Eliezer Papo, *Pele' Yo'etz* (Jerusalem: Shmuel Zukerman Press, 1903), part 2, 29b.

for generations in an artificial incubator, in which we could grow and cultivate values that were not put to the test of reality." But those same "values and content of consciousness" are needed today more than in the past. Some of them, like the idea of restraining one's power, stemmed precisely from looking at power and the response to it. In my understanding, the attempt to imitate God, act patiently and with restraint and not out of pride or vengeance, is more relevant today than in the past, precisely because we have so much power. Moreover, the value of patience is not one of restraint alone. That is, patience is not only the foregoing of action. It is a struggle against a type of thinking that sees actions that involve force and are carried out with vengeance, pride, and self-honor as positive or necessary. And this is my second point of contention with Yeshayahu Leibowitz.

In the most challenging sentence of Leibowitz's response to Qibya, he claims that an act of vengeance is cursed even though it is justified. In justifying the military operation, Ariel Sharon, the officer in charge, argued that the goal achieved was the "puncturing of the myth of the unconquerable Arab village." It was a vengeful, murderous act undertaken in the name of honor and deterrence. A response that creates a balance of fear, creating deterrence and vengeance, seems to Leibowitz as both justified and cursed. But, as I understand our tradition, this action was not justified. To be more precise, there is no justification for a Jew taking part in such an operation because Jews are forbidden to take revenge. The action was not cursed; it was forbidden.

The literal meaning of the verses in the story of Shechem also points in a similar direction. Shimon and Levi's massacre is not justified yet cursed; it is unjustified and therefore forbidden. And more broadly, "actions" are not cursed in the story of Shechem. People are cursed because they sinned. Understanding that murdering out of vengeance or a desire for honor or pride is not "justified but cursed" but, rather, unjustified and therefore forbidden is an understanding that requires listening to our Jewish tradition. Other traditions see violence for deterrence or preserving one's honor as justified and sometimes suitable behavior. One example of this kind of ethical tradition is that of Sharon and Unit 101. To oppose this emerging tradition, opposition based upon the tradition of "the patient study-house" is necessary.

Traditional Jews of my grandfather's generation, shocked by the state's power and confused by their new lives, withdrew into their homes. This is how a rich ethical-religious world was temporarily lost, while a new interpretation that distorted Jewish texts and subordinates them to the state grew in its place. The requirement that I leave my Jewish values at home is impossible. It is not in line with my Judaism, mainly when the state acts according to moral standards that oppose Jewish tradition—sometimes in the name of this very tradition. Patience is needed today more than ever. As the author of *Orchot Tzaddikim* writes in his fifteenth-century work of musar, "Many good branches stem from the root of humility: the humble person is patient, and from patience will come peace. And humility will silence the anger of a person who is angry at him, as it says (Proverbs 15:1), 'a gentle response assuages wrath.' And peace is an excellent value." [27]

---

27 *Orhot Tzadikim* (Jerusalem: Eshkol Library Publishing, 1977), 32.

3

Submission

If you see a person prophesizing about the Messiah, know that [...] it will end in shame and disgrace for the whole world [...]. And secrets and accounts are taught to him for his shame and the shame of those who believe his words.[1]

—Yehuda HeHhasid, *Sefer Hasidim* (Germany, thirteenth century)

Religious Zionism in Israel—A Religious-National State of the Union

Sometimes it's hard to see the rigidity of Religious Zionism's political boundaries, mainly because there is a remarkable increase in the movement's openness in other areas. For example, contemporary Religious Zionism allows for differences in religious self-expression. There are now extensive creative spiritual works: Religious Zionist poetry and contemplative, fictional works on the relationship between people and God. In many regards, the Religious Zionist community allows, and even supports, intellectual independence. In specific sectors, including my own community, there are more ways for women to participate in religious life than there were in the past (for example, learning Torah) and more egalitarian prayer services. While there is still a long way to go, LGBT is being normalized in some liberal sectors. More so, children of Religious Zionists have integrated into secular society. Religious newscasters, judges, and other public figures have become common. Religious communities are less closed off. There is no doubt that Religious Zionism is more diverse today than it ever was in the past. Some even claim that its conservative and liberal branches are on the brink of splitting into two separate movements. However, there is one area where uniformity of opinion still reigns and minimal discussion space is still the norm: the question of the meaning, religious centrality, and political

---

1 Judah the Pious, *Sefer Hasidim*, ed. R. Margoliouth, (Jerusalem, Mossad ha-Rav Kook, 1957), sec. 206, 195.

implications of Israeli nationalism. Moreover, most Religious Zionists think that the most genuine expression of religious nationalism is aggressive Jewish supremacy—religion in service of the state.

There are hardly any religious voices today challenging the idea that Jewish citizens matter more than Arab citizens. There is no public position within the Religious Zionist community advocating for an end to the occupation on religious grounds. Perhaps one can most clearly see this uniformity of opinion in the Religious Zionist community's adoration of and reverence for the Israeli military. All Religious Zionist communities, whether conservative or liberal, prepare their students for the army. The most prominent Religious Zionist representatives in the Knesset—from liberals to the radical right—all pride themselves on impressive military pasts. There is an argument within the community over whether religious women should serve in the army, but no one casts doubt on the spiritual importance of military service. Conservative community members insist that only men should join the military, while Religious Zionist centrists argue that men and women should serve. Ultimately, this aggressive nationalism is characteristic of all Religious Zionism. The movement has willfully submitted itself to the state's nationalist logic.

In recent years, this nationalism has moved rightwards, a direction wholly supported and sometimes spearheaded by Religious Zionism. All the younger generations of Religious Zionists identify as right-wing and advocate for Israeli control over the entire Land of Israel. Yes, all of them. A poll conducted by the *Makor Rishon* newspaper in 2018 discovered how many young Religious Zionists identify as leftists. The answer was zero.[2] How many of them identified as center-left? Again, zero. Only 4% defined themselves as centrists, while over 90% located themselves on the right of the political spectrum, the majority of whom described themselves as being on the hard right rather than the mainstream right or center-right. These inclinations are more extreme among the younger generation, but the same trend is valid for all Religious Zionism. In their book *Israeli Judaism*, Shmuel Rosner and Camille Fox explain that just 1% of those who identify as Religious Zionists define themselves as strongly left.[3]

---

2   "Poll: Voting Trends among Young Religious Zionists," *Maqor Rishon,* June 15, 2018. Hebrew.

3   Shmuel Rosner and Camil Fuchs, *Yahadut Yisraelit: Diyukan shel mahapekhat tarbutit* (Jerusalem: Jewish People Policy Institute, 2018), 242.

Why Not Leave?

If Religious Zionism won't accept my religious position, why am I still part of it? The answer is: because a person who wants to live an Orthodox life needs a community—a synagogue, teachers for one's children. It is impossible to live as a religious individual without a congregation. And so, a person must decide which community to be part of. Although the State of Israel appears to have many different types of communities, there are only two options for a religious Jew. To give a rough breakdown, an Orthodox person in Israel must decide between belonging to the ultra-Orthodox or the Religious Zionist community. There are, of course, many subcommunities, but these two communities are the overarching frameworks for religious life in Israel. In Israel there are four separate education systems: a secular system, an Arab system, a religious Zionist system, and an ultra-Orthodox (Haredi) system. One has to choose a community in order to decide the framework in which one's children will be educated. Even religious people who hold opinions that do not align with either of these two options need to join one of these communities if they want to educate their children in a religious framework.

The norms and religious culture of Haredi society try to hold modernity at bay, and being a member of the Haredi community is, therefore, impossible for me to consider. I wish to be part of a larger world, rather than closed off in my religious community; I want gender equality, and have an interest in literature and knowledge about the world beyond Jewish texts—all of these commitments prevent me from being part of Haredi society. I must emphasize that these are religious reasons. I do not think that people can live God-fearing lives when they are isolated and do not participate in public discourse. I cannot accept Haredi seclusion from the knowledge of the world. Of course, not all Haredim are like this. In recent years (and before that as well), new voices are speaking out about gender, economic equality, and even civil equality. But, as a rule, the Haredi educational institutions don't hold those positions. And just as I grew up in the Religious Zionist world and see it as the community I belong to, they see themselves as part of the Haredi community.

Because of this, the Religious Zionism community is the only one I can consider. This has implications. My children go to Religious Zionist schools and youth movements. We pray at a Religious Zionist synagogue. Although we are at the liberal end of the community, we are still part of it. The price I pay for belonging to Religious Zionism is political loneliness. I assume that the vast majority of Religious Zionists would not see me as part of their community. Many Religious Zionists would not think that a person who calls for an end to control over millions of Palestinians could represent a legitimate position in the community. But I need one. I need a synagogue.

The Frustrating Relationship between Religious Obligation and Right-Wing Positions in Religious Zionism

Because I am a part of the Religious Zionist community, I am particularly troubled by its views, especially the close connection it insists upon between religious obligation and Jewish supremacy and aggression. Religious duty, on the one hand, and belief in the occupation and Jewish superiority, on the other, are tightly linked in Israel. Religious Zionism asserts that to be religious means being right-wing: it is impossible to accept one without the other.

However, my political views do not compromise ethical obligations and religious obligations. My opposition to Israel's control over other people against their will does not stem from spiritual weakness or uncertainty. My political views do not testify to a lack of obligation to traditional sources. They make me reject blind allegiance to the state and oppose the use of force without cause. In other words, I don't hold a position compromising between Religious Zionism and universalism; I firmly oppose the central theology of Religious Zionism, which privileges the state above all else and sees it as the religious center. Such a perspective is also common among, perhaps even key for, Religious Zionist "moderates." They sanctify the army much more than those on the extreme right. For example, the extreme right is much more likely to support opposing or refusing military orders than the moderate camp.

As time goes on, it has become harder to articulate a dissenting position within Religious Zionism. There are many reasons for its rightward drift and theological narrowing. However, there is one reason in particular that I want to discuss: the hope for redemption that didn't come.

Messianic Reality

The Zionist movement was established by nonreligious people (even if Religious Zionists took part in it from its earliest days). Zionist thinkers, both on the left and the right, including Herzl, Ahad Ha'am, Borochov, and Jabotinsky, saw the movement as nonreligious, and even antireligious. It aspired, like many national ideologies, to "redeem" the people and turn them into a "normal" nation, governed not by God but by a flesh and blood ruler. Secular Zionist thinkers believed that if they removed God from the Jewish political equation, the Jewish nation would become sovereign, like all nations.[4]

Although the Zionist movement worked to realize a secular-nationalist vision, it borrowed the language of the national redemption of the Jewish people from religious texts. The very concepts of "redemption" and "exile" are central anchors of the Zionist movement.[5] Secular Zionists "redeemed" the land and called for the "ingathering of the exiles" to establish and build the State of Israel, employing the word "aliyah" (literally, ascent). They referred to meaningful events in Zionist history as "miracles." They dreamed of establishing a state which would restore the "kingdom of Israel." This language allowed Religious Zionists to feel that they belonged and that the secular Zionist project was, at its core, a national religious project. But Religious Zionism's idea of redemption was always different from that of the secular Zionist establishment.

Secular Redemption?

Although secular Zionism's language is saturated with a longing for redemption, the question remains: How can modern nationalism be theologically squared with halakha? Religious Zionism had to translate the secular Zionist belief in the "beginning of redemption" into halakhic language. It is important to note that this was a *translation*, not a return to a traditional source. There have been many expressions of messianic mysticism in Jewish texts throughout history, but a modern state is, by definition, a secular project. It derives its authority from the consent the world's nations and its citizens, and it acts within a world of rules designed not in the beit midrash but outside of it.

Traditional Jews see divine intervention as a necessary condition for their redemption. In opposition to this viewpoint, secular Zionist ideology rejected

---

4   As Shlomo Aviner writes: "Zionism isn't a linear continuation of messianic Jewish desire. Rather, it is a modern and revolutionary ideology, symbolizing a clear break from a passive messianic faith that thinks redemption will appear through divine intervention. Moses Hess and Pinsker, Herzl and Nordau, Borokhov and Jabotinsky—all of them believed in the intelligence of the secularized Jew, "most often assimilated." See "Zionism and Jewish Religious Tradition: Dialectics of Redemption and Secularization," in *Tziyyonut ve-dat*, ed. A. Shapira, Y. Reinharz, and S. Almog (Jerusalem: Shazar Center, 1994), 11.

5   Much has been written about this dynamic, including, famously, by Gershom Scholem to Franz Rosenzweig in 1926: "No words are just created, but rather taken from our 'old and good' treasures, filled to the brim with explosive power." Gershom Scholem, *Devarim be-go* (Tel Aviv: Am Oved, 1989), 59–60. My translation.

the expectation of intervention from above, portraying it as characteristic of Diasporic "passivity." Religious Zionist rabbis thus needed to reconcile the explicit contradiction between secular Zionism, which seemingly rejected any necessity for divine intervention, and the traditional approach founded upon this very necessity. Moreover, these rabbis also had to contend with a position that had developed in the traditional world, according to which Jews were forbidden to build a Jewish kingdom in Israel that did not result from a miraculous process.[6] Thus, Religious Zionism, in a boldly new interpretation, declared that Zionist activities were part of redemption. However, the problem lay not in naming the particular moment or period as the time of redemption but instead in identifying a secular movement as the harbinger of redemption. After Religious Zionist rabbis declared that this was a historical moment that heralded redemption, they had to give an account of secular nationalism as an essential and legitimate part of a significant religious moment.

At the center of the Zionist project was not the service of God but rather the Jewish people themselves, with no connection to God. The project oscillated between indifference to religion and active opposition to traditional religious ideas while at the same time using religious language for its purposes. It wanted to free the Jewish people from subjugation to God. Different and diverse answers were given to the question of Zionism, but one response was not among them: "sanctifying God's name and performing religious commandments." From the perspective of Zionist thinkers, not only were the rabbis a relic of the past but so was their God. Rejecting God and God's authority was not an unexpected outcome of Zionism, then, but one of its foundational precepts. Early Religious Zionist rabbis understood the challenge facing them and tried to oppose Zionist secularism while simultaneously redeeming it.

The Zionist Answer to the Question "Why Were We Exiled?"

The Zionist movement told Jewish history anew in order to replace the rabbinic version the Jewish story. According to the standard Zionist narrative, the Jewish

---

6   Of course many Jews lived and immigrated to Israel/Palestine since the destruction of the Second Temple. The Mishna and the Jerusalem Talmud were written in Israel, as well as many texts throughout the middle ages. To read more on religious attitudes opposed to the building of the State of Israel, see Menachem Friedman, "The Attitude of Religious Circles to the Establishment of Israel: A Clear Instance of 'The Return to History,'" in *Ha-Tziyyonut ve-ha-ḥazarah le-historiyah*, ed. S. N. Eisenstadt and Moshe Lissak (Jerusalem: Yad Ben Zvi, 1999), 447–464.

people during its two thousand years of exile. Archaic religious traditions led Jews to abstain from political power struggles and were thus the reason for the people's political weakness in the Diaspora. The traditional religious story, in which Israel's exile was a punishment for violating the covenant it had entered into with God, was substituted with a secular-nationalist tale about a nation that had lost its greatness because of its helplessness—one which should now arise and reclaim its power. In both versions of the narrative, the people were exiled from their land. Still, according to the traditional Jewish view, exile results from our sins, namely political zealousness, and national pride.

In a famous series of aggadic stories in the Talmudic tractate of Gittin (56a), the rabbis explain why the Second Temple was destroyed and the religious meaning of the destruction. In this account, there were two groups within the city. The rabbis, represented by Rabban Yohanan Ben Zakkai, were ready to surrender to the Romans to safeguard Jerusalem and the Torah; they were opposed by Jewish thugs who wanted to fight the Romans out of zealous national pride. These same thugs burned the city's grain storehouses to force all Jews to fight. But burning the warehouses led to starvation and death.

This story, and many others like it, show that, according to the rabbis, the destruction of the Temple was not the result of weakness but aggressive nationalism. Not only do the rabbis see national pride as unimportant, but they see zealousness itself as the cause of the Temple's destruction. Humility and patience are not weaknesses but are lessons to be learned from the tale.

Contrary to this narrative, the Zionist story depicts political weakness as a sin; perhaps even subordination to God is a sin. It sees exile as the result of Jewish weakness, and this weakness must be changed. Zionists transformed characters that Jewish tradition had tried to forget time and time again, such as the people of Masada and Bar Kochba, and refashioned them as positive examples of those who took their fate into their own hands. Those who had sanctified the name of Heaven throughout history and died as martyrs were seen as passive victims who prevented the return to history. According to the central narratives of traditional Judaism, to repent for a sin it is necessary to understand the wrongdoing and regret it. In addition, one must reassess one's values and commitments, act in service of God, and seek spiritual guidance. Repentance also requires dialogue with God, the outcome of which one cannot know in advance. Zionism, however, decided that the great Jewish sin was political, and that to fix it the Jews needed new political instincts, pride, and weapons. As a result, religious Zionists joined the Zionist movement and, in doing so, gave up on the traditional view of history and the idea that repentance is crucial for redemption.

Zionism tried to create a new national structure without a religious communal framework that puts God at its center. It entirely opposed the cooperative system Jews had lived in for hundreds of years. However, the state is a civil body that receives its authority from the majority's will. Therefore, rejecting God's sovereignty is not only a statement of faith but also a political statement. Only denying God's power allows the State of Israel to be sovereign. It is difficult, then, to understand how a Jewish religious movement could join a Jewish political movement whose entire essence contradicted rabbinic Judaism and the acceptance of divine sovereignty.

Two Religious Justifications for Zionism and Transience as a Solution

Religious Jews who wanted to justify and adopt Zionism had two options, two paths by which to justify Zionism from a theological perspective, one tragic and the other innovative and optimistic. The tragic position saw Zionism as a political answer to antisemitism and the danger Jews suffered from. The tragedy of this view was in accepting the necessity of Zionism's existence, even though it rebelled against the tradition and God. This position does not assume that Zionism is a step toward redemption. The state, in this view, is a political necessity and therefore must be supported. Religious people in such a community must preserve their faith and ancestors' traditions and influence other Jews to become more religiously observant. Among those who held this opinion included those who defined themselves as Zionists and those who did not. For example, the early Mizrahi leader, Rabbi Yitzhak Yaakov Reines, saw Zionism as solely political. Rabbi Yosef David HaLevi Soloveitchik (1903-1993) took part in leading the Mizrahi movement, yet he was ambivalent about the redemptive aspect of Zionism.[7] Rabbi Ovadia Yosef (1920-2013) also had a complicated relationship with the movement.[8] On the one hand, he saw Israel as a place where the world of the Torah could flourish (and even save Jews from antisemitism), but he also saw secularization and secularism as real threats.

The second way Zionism was justified from a religious perspective was completely different. This position, whose central thinker was Rabbi Abraham

---

7   For further analysis of Rabbi Soloveitchik's complex attitude to Zionism, see, for example, Aaron Lichtenstein, "On Rav Soloveitck's Attitude Towards Zionism," *Alon Shvut Bogrim* 16 (2002): 157–171.

8   See Ariel Picard, *Mishnato shel R. Ovadya Yofef be-eidan shel temurot* (Ramat-Gan: Bar-Ilan University, 2007), 149–194.

Isaac HaKohen Kook, adopted the messianic fervor of Zionism and other national movements and saw the national process as metaphysical-religious and independent of the intentions of those who led it.[9] In his view, what appeared as a rebellion against God's sovereignty was actually an act of following God's desire and purpose. Over many years, this position became dominant, especially among the leading rabbis of Religious Zionism.

As the foundation of the state neared, the gap between a modern state and religious halakhic rule became more tangible. The concept of citizenship is modern, as are parliamentary democracy, civil rights, sovereignty, and the essence of the word "state." Nevertheless, halakhah was not constructed when these concepts were in use, and therefore the terms "halakhic state" or "Jewish state" required new and innovative halakhic interpretations. The contradictions between the profane and the holy, between the modern and the premodern, were often too blunt.

One of the ways to deal with the gaps between Religious Zionist interpretations of the halakhic and state's positions was to see the Zionist movement and the secular nation as a transitional stage. In such a reality, the role of Religious Zionism was to justify, for lack of another option, the status quo, while declaring its desire for change. Rabbi Yitzhak HaLevi Herzog exemplifies this type of thinking, especially in his grappling with the idea of equal citizenship.

The Logic of Transience in National Halakha (Hilkhot Tzibur)

In 1946, the Anglo-American Committee of Inquiry visited Palestine. Its task was to determine the feasibility of Jewish and Palestinian sovereignty in the area. The delegation met different groups and learned about various views in the Jewish settlement in Palestine. One of the central voices was Rabbi Yitzhak HaLevi Herzog, the chief rabbi of the Mandate-era settlement and Rabbi Kook's successor. When the state was founded, Rabbi Herzog was appointed as its chief Ashkenazi rabbi, a position in which he served until he died. He was asked to write a public statement for the committee explaining how a religious stance could be squared with a Western secularism, according to which sovereignty is in the hands of the people and not in the hands of God.

---

9   See for example Abraham Isaac Kook, *Orot* (Jerusalem: Mossad Harav Kook, 1921).

Rabbi Herzog wrote unambiguously that the State of Israel would be a democracy and that Arab minority rights would be preserved, like the rights of any minority in any democratic state. The state would be of the Jews, Rabbi Herzog wrote in English, but it would be a state like all other states.[10] In parallel to his public statement, he also published a book called *Techukah leYisrael Al Pi HaTorah*. It is written in the style of responsa literature and attempts to bridge the gap between the concept of a Jewish halakhic state and a liberal democratic state. Thus he writes at the beginning of the book:

> The work imposed upon me by the full assembly council of the Chief Rabbinate of Israel is both important and challenging. I do not praise myself in my heart that I have succeeded in solving all of these problems when the truth is that until this point, I have not been so blessed. My main goal was to show that it is possible to create legislation for a Jewish state and establish a legal regime that would not contradict our holy Torah in any detail. We should, in my opinion, aim with all of our might towards this goal. Because if, God forbid, we were to become lax in the service of Heaven, at this decisive moment, God forbid, that the great rabbi of the *Yishuv* would give up, God forbid, on the Torah and would adopt, without considering our holy Torah, which roots our souls, some ready-made, modern, gentile legislation, some Swiss legal code or something, and this on its own would already be its complete internal destruction—spiritual-religious-historical—and a great desecration in the face of the outside world.
>
> It seems that it is enough to say these harsh words without clarifying them. May it be God's will that the Lord imbues the work of our hands and that the light of Torah illuminates the hearts of all of our brethren in Israel and the Diaspora, and that we may merit the entire Jewish state speedily of the dawn of redemption, in the spirit of the Torah, built upon its foundations, and from here to full redemption, amen, amen![11]

---

10 Herzog's letter to the Anglo-American Committee of Inquiry can be found here: https://upload.wikimedia.org/wikipedia/commons/thumb/e/ec/Herzog_To_Anglo-American_Committee_of_Inquiry.pdf/page1-587px-Herzog_To_Anglo-American_Committee_of_Inquiry.pdf.jpg. Accessed 22 May 2023.

11 Isaac Halevi Herzog, *Techukah le-Yisrael 'al pi ha-Torah,* (Jerusalem: Mossad Harav Kook, 1988), 11. Concerning R. Herzog's views on the constitution of the Jewish state, see

Rabbi Herzog claims here that it is impossible to establish a state according to Jewish law in the current political conditions. The principles of Jewish law contradict the principles of the kind of state the other nations of the world would allow us to create. In the present reality, he contends, it is thus only possible to remain an involved party in running the state (Rabbi Herzog was selected to be the chief rabbi of the state). Religious people, then, must help to mold the state in accordance with Jewish law to the extent possible. Rabbi Herzog could not convince the world's nations to agree to establish a halakhic state. Still, he believed that it was possible to establish a state that, even if it did not act according to Torah, would at least not be founded on "some ready-made, modern, gentile legislation."

Herzog's position is grounded upon a constant negotiation between what is desirable from a nationalist-religious perspective and what is possible to obtain from a nationalist-secular position. His willingness to engage in these negotiations and sometimes to act in opposition to Jewish law came from his belief that this was a temporary constraint. But if his position allowed for equal citizenship to sufficiently please the outside world, what did he see as genuinely ideal? What did he think was a suitable relationship with Arab citizens?

The Temporariness of "Beginnings"

In one of the chapters in *Techukah leYisrael*, Rabbi Herzog considers how to reconcile a modern, civil regime, in which all citizens have equal rights, with premodern halakha, which entails a religious-ethnic hierarchy that is built into Jewish rule.[12] For premodern rabbinic thought, modern, equal citizenship did not yet exist. One of the categories of a non-Jew who lived under Jewish rule was a *ger toshav* (resident alien).[13] Resident aliens had partial rights: they could live in the Land of Israel (as mentioned, the concept of a sovereign state did not yet exist) but had a lower status than Jews. For example, they could not buy land and could not offer all the sacrifices. Rabbi Herzog translated this premodern reality to the State of Israel and argued that non-Jews in the country (who

---

Alexander Kaye, *The Invention of Jewish Theocracy: The Struggle for Legal Authority in Modern Israel* (Oxford: Oxford University Press 2020).

12 Isaac Halevi Herzog, "Gentiles in the Jewish State," in *Reshut: Teshuvot mevo'arot mi-gedolei ha-Posqim benei zemaneinu* (Jerusalem: Reuben Mass, 2008).

13 For further reading on the conceptual development of "resident aliens" in rabbinic literature, see Adi Ophir and Ishay Rosen Zvi, *Goy: Israel's Multiple Others and the Birth of the Gentile* (Oxford: Oxford University Press, 2018), 180–182.

had not declared themselves as enemies) were included under the category of ger toshav.

While defining Arabs who live in Israel as "resident aliens" did indeed square with halakha, it implied unequal citizenship. So how did Rabbi Herzog contend with the halakhic problem created by his attempt to combine a modern nation-state with adherence to premodern principles? Without the possibility of solving the basic contradiction between defining citizenship in a modern, sovereign state and premodern halakha, Rabbi Herzog needed the halakhic concept of "when Israel does not have full power": the nations of the world will not let us create a state in which Jews have preferred status, and so, therefore, in the meantime, we must give all of the state's residents equal citizenship. The phrase indeed appears in Maimonides's *Laws of Idol Worship* (10:6) but it is a completely foreign concept to modern nationalism, in which states derive their legitimacy from the international community.[14] But Rabbi Herzog preferred to receive international agreement to establish the State of Israel, hoping that one day the state would act according to halakha and grant exceptional standing to Jewish citizens—that is, discriminate against its Arab citizens.

What Rabbi Herzog thought had to happen for the State of Israel to act according to halakha is unclear. He wrote his responsum in 1946, before the state was established. However, his proposed structure of legitimizing a secular democratic regime as a temporary solution, has multiple implications. One implication is that civil equality is an injustice requiring correction. Eliminating equality is, in fact, the telos in which the state should be headed.

Voices in the moderate Religious Zionism world might say that the long-term goals of Rabbi Herzog and his camp are irrelevant. At the end of the day, they would argue, his religious position *allows* for democracy and civil equality, even if it is not, in essence, democratic. I fear that this claim does not seriously consider his position's theological and educational implications. Even if Religious Zionism is prepared to live with a measure of equality in practice, it is important to understand that the movement doesn't want this reality but rather sees it as a necessary compromise. Rabbi Herzog's theology aspires toward a Jewish halakhic state. In his ideal halakhic state, Jews are the only sovereign citizens. The state would control all the land of biblical Israel and have sovereignty over all of it; and the state would disregard the laws of war agreed upon by the international community, instead acting according to halakhic war laws.

---

14 Moses Maimonides, *Mishneh Torah, Laws of Idol Worship* 1:10.

Other rabbis agreed with Rabbi Herzog. Rabbi Shaul Yisraeli, mentioned above in reference to his halakhic ruling on the Qibya massacre, explained his vision of the halakhic project in an interview with the newspaper *HaTzofe*:

> At this point, we are in a battle from all sides. We are fighting against two positions whose conclusions are entirely opposed to one another, yet both of them share a point of departure: they do not believe in the possibility of building normal, political life according to the Torah; they think that the only place for the Torah is in a miracle state, whose existence is a constantly revealed miracle. According to this opinion, a Jewish state can only stem out of the laws of the Torah. According to this opinion, there is no solution to the problem of Shabbat, and the imposition of religion in daily life is impossible unless it is the kingdom of the kingly Messiah. Therefore, one position, which emphasizes the Torah and only the Torah, concludes that it is impossible that this state which we arrived at with all of the present facts, with the same population make-up and type of regime, and according to a natural process of "the world keeps turning," that this state would be from Heaven and according to the Torah of the beginning of redemption. Therefore this state is hurrying up the messianic era, and faithful Judaism must have nothing to do with this. On the other hand, the second position emphasizes the state and believes that, with regards to the state, one must give up on the values of halakha, which were given only as the foundation for individual life and not for communal life. These two positions leave no space for inquiry into state problems from the perspective of halakha.

Thus, our position opposes both of these views regarding an appraisal of the state and the capacity of the Torah's laws. In our opinion, the state is the revelation of divine grace, as the beginning of the ascent towards complete redemption. Therefore, it is forbidden for us to look apathetically at everything happening in it. Even if we succeed in closing ourselves off, we see the obligation to direct the state towards the path of faithfulness and to strive for this incessantly. Even if the goal seems far, we believe that the Torah is the Torah of life. Halakha does not diminish the state's steps. On the contrary, halakha's power and ability can direct the state's way of life, creating a Jewish form that will raise its value and acquire it a most honorable place among the nations.[15]

Rabbi Yisraeli admits that Religious Zionism's halakhic challenges are the product of coercion. Our tradition does not force us to see Israel's reality as miraculous or judge it as so. A Jew can believe that the Israeli project has no connection to redemption or religious meaning. The matter that Rabbi Herzog deliberated over regarding the status of Jews and Arabs within the State of Israel was the result of deciding that the modern state is the foundation for the future messianic kingdom. If the State of Israel is not the beginning of redemption, there need not be an aspiration toward future inequality.

And if someone argues that "in any vision of redemption, there will be inequality between Jews and Arabs," one must answer that it is not the case. Such a statement itself entails capitulation to the internal logic of the modern state. Inequality is not built into the Jewish vision of redemption; it stems, rather, from subjugating a messianic idea to contemporary thinking.

Civil inequality is the result of civil standing. If the vision of redemption is not subordinated to the discourse of the modern state, then at the least, it does not have to contend with the problems that the boundaries of this discourse create. Modern civic logic is built upon a paradigm of power, control, sovereignty, and territory that make sense only at this moment in history. However, the logic of redemption does not require us to contend with the problems created by Religious Zionism. Instead, it allows us to hope for a radically different time, with different logical paradigms. It is indeed hard to imagine the world to come while still living in this one. But imagination is not a problem of religious: it is a feature built into it.[16] While we do not know how to imagine God, it does not mean we do not talk about or with God. Religious Zionism needs to make the imagination of redemption shallow enough for this political moment, a random in human history, and declare: "This is redemption!" This is a renunciation of traditional religious imagination. Religious Zionism submits to the logic of the state rather than to religious motivation. Doing so reduces its thinking—and, indeed, religious thought as a whole—to the boundaries of the secular state. As time passes and complete redemption does not arrive, Religious Zionism intensifies this same intellectual and halakhic capitulation.

Religious Zionism was founded upon a compromise and upon the assumption that the secular state was "a state in the process." But as the years have passed, the claim that Israeli Secularism is temporary has become increasingly

---

15 Rabbi Shaul Yisraeli, "The Editor and the Appraiser," *Hatzofeh*, 1 July, 1955.

16 A different approach to reconciling power and redemption is presented in chapter 4.

dubious. Time has passed, and the sovereign state has gotten stronger; but the end of days is yet to occur. The youth of today's Religious Zionism are the first generation that understands, even if not explicitly, that the process of redemption will continue for a long time, and its end cannot be known. This delayed redemption has strengthened two positions within contemporary Religious Zionism.

The "When We Are in Power" Approach: On Brutish Religious Zionism

Tired of waiting for a redemption that tarries, part of the Religious Zionist leadership made a decision: If what is preventing the realization of redemption is the fact that "we are not in power," then we must assert our power. Those who support the "when we are in power" approach maintain that a believing Jew does not need to pray for divine intervention but rather to declare that the time of redemption has arrived. Members of brutish Religious Zionism are not frustrated by God, who has not responded to Zionist action. They are frustrated by the state, which is not sufficiently Jewish in their view. Even if the leaders of the "when we are in power" approach are very religious, their political worldview is clearly secular. The brutes of Religious Zionism don't see any need for God's intervention. They can achieve their goal by themselves.

It is no wonder that words such as "sovereignty," "control," and "occupation" are granted special status by those who hold this view. They require that God's messengers, meaning the State of Israel or themselves, carry out the commandment of "revenge." There is no need for the Holy of Holies on the Temple Mount; there is a need instead for "sovereignty" on the Temple Mount. There is no need for the Messiah to come; there is a need instead for "applying sovereignty over the entire territory of Judea and Samaria." The "when we are in power" school of thought requires the imposition of God's will through brutish, human violence. They do not desire God's sovereignty but rather human autonomy. When Rabbi Eliezer Melamed, for example, was asked about his position about ascending the Temple Mount, he said he permitted it, explaining that "there is especially a value in doing so in this period, when there is a utility in ascending, to preserve our sovereignty there."[17]

---

17 Eliezer Melamed, "Ask the Rabbi," yeshiva.org, accessed 22 May 2023, https://www.yeshiva.org.il/ask/184.

A decade ago, very few Jews ascended the Temple Mount. Almost all decisors forbid the ascent, as it is a holy place which requires special purification rituals which are irrelevant without the existence of the Temple. Building the Temple, reinstating the Sanhedrin, and offering animal sacrifices were always considered "messianic halakhah"—halakhic matters that will be adjudicated during the End of Days, but not in the current reality. Yet even though the Messiah has not arrived, prominent Religious Zionists today call for ascending the Temple Mount and praying there—and many make this ascent.[18]

The call to ascend the Temple Mount is no less important than the ascent itself. In the summer of 2017, the joint staff of the Temple Mount Movement, an Israeli organization that encourages ascending the Temple Mount, published a video.[19] In the video, a young man is shown wearing a knit kippah on his head and sidelocks behind his ears. He explains that ascending the Temple Mount is permissible by Jewish law in clear and straightforward language. Yes, the energetic spokesperson admits, only those who have undergone ritual immersion can ascend the mount, and one must also know where it is permitted and where it is forbidden to stand. "But why should we involved ourselves with all of these issues?" he asks as if speaking about an annoying homework assignment. "We won't buy the Temple Mount in the grocery store or take it out of a warehouse ready made. We will take over the Mount with our bodies... there is a commandment of Occupying." To the sound of secular Zionist Naomi Shemer's "Yibaneh HaMikdash" (The Temple Will Be Built), the narrator declares, "Dear friends, the Temple Mount is the symbol of control over the land. As Uri Zvi Greenberg wrote, whoever controls the Temple Mount, controls the land."

The video expresses Religious Zionism's identification with secular Zionism's "activism," which doesn't wait for God but takes its fate into its own hands. Israel is already no longer just a step on the path to redemption but redemption itself. This development within Religious Zionism distances it even further from traditional religiosity. Religious Zionist activism is not new. Establishing settlements is a form of activism. Yet the building of the Temple Mount is not activism to speed up a future redemption, but rather to complete the process, without God's presence. God's involvement is no longer needed, even in sacred matters. However, pushing God out of the equation,

---

18 See for example the call of prominent rabbis, including Rabbis Elyakim Levanon, Haim Ratig, and Eliyahu Blum, to ascend to the Temple Mount. The letter was reported in Reut Hadar, "Call From Rabbis in Favor of Ascending in Purity to Temple Mount," *Arutz Sheva,* December 27, 2014, https://www.inn.co.il/news/288222.

19 Taken from a video filmed by the Joint Headquarters for the Temple Mount (an assembly of organizations dedicated to Jewish sovereignty on Temple Mount: https://www.youtube.com/channel/UC7sr4uHn1aXSdO4stYBB-Lw.

and replacing Him with political activism, is a negation of religion, even if it the process is run by God fearing individuals. The Jewish state is secular, and according to this school of thought, then, the ultimate expression of religiosity is the demonstration of the state's sovereignty.

Completing redemption with brute force hasn't succeeded, and there is no reason to believe it will triumph in the future. It doesn't matter how many days of learning or practice sessions young priests engage in, how much land the Israeli government annexes, or how many religious nation-state laws are advanced. The failure will be double: this theopolitical fantasy cannot be realized.

Sadly, until this is understood, militarist religious culture will continue to influence our religious world. This culture will continue to admire what is coarse and combative, the absence of humility, and extreme violence. We must be cautious of the "when we are in power" school, as they are the enemy of traditional Jewish ethics. The tradition teaches us that the conversation with God is a dialogue that opens through performing mitzvot and not a monologue of belligerent decisions. When we pray to God, we make requests of Him; we do not report to Him on what we have executed.

The replacement of the Jew who speaks with God with the Jew who makes declarations in God's name exemplifies the erasure of the rabbinic ethical model. To approach God, we must accept that it is not in our power to know how, if at all, we will be answered. Those who speak in God's name lose their ability to hear and see. They cannot see the suffering that they cause or the sadness they bring about. Their blindness prevents them from seeing the beauty in compassion and the possibility that redemption in this world is an act of spiritual elevation and not an act of aggression.

Israeli Judaism: Tradition as Domesticated Culture for the Benefit of the State

The "when we have power" approach declares that the time for redemption has come, even without God's intervention. Another system within contemporary Religious Zionism claims that we have left exile, but redemption in its religious-political sense is no longer critical.[20] Supporters of this view favor a new "Israeli Judaism" as a substitute for the rabbinic world of halakha, which, they believe, is

---

20 This outlook has developed immensely over the last years. For an overview, history, and analysis, see Mikhael Manekin, "Two Approaches to Israeli Judaism," *Hazman Hazeh*, accessed 22 May 2023, https://www.haaretz.co.il/hazmanhazeh/2021-11-04/ty-article-magazine/0000017f-ed2c-d0f7-a9ff-efed32ae0000.

no longer relevant. The secular Israeli reality is not temporary but permanent. It is not a vestibule leading to redemption but the place itself. This is a new perspective within Religious Zionism. Still, it adopts a well-known concept from secular Zionism: the idea of the new Jew, who lives in the Land of Israel and practices a contemporary Judaism.

One of the main representatives of Israeli Judaism is Dr. Micah Goodman.[21] He is an alumnus of liberal Religious Zionist institutions, and in his book *The Wondering Jew* he notes that he sends his children to these same institutions. In recent years, he has published two books whose goals are to try and find "an Israeli middle path," as he puts it. The first book, *Catch '67*, tries to reconcile the his version of the right and the left with regards to the occupation. The second book, *The Wondering Jew*, attempts to contend with the split between the religious and secular worlds.

The Wondering Jew is very personal. Goodman shares his misgivings with the reader. He is a talented writer, able to present complex ideas simply and convincingly. He toggles between secular and religious perspectives and tries to identify the fundamental elements that should be preserved, distinguishing between those, on the one hand, and the parts that should be abandoned, on the other.

Goodman identifies two contemporary tensions in Israel. In his view, religious tension in the modern state is due to a lack of criticalness, which stems from halakha, a legal system that subjugates the individual to a daily routine of services and rituals that creates a perpetual feeling of guilt and an inability to judge reality. An additional source of religious tension, Goodman argues, is the discord between the sacred world of values and the modern Western world of values—for example, in matters related to gender. According to Goodman, "secularism" also creates strain. It is individualistic and detaches people from communal belonging that leads to existential depression.

Goodman lives in the religious world, but, he claims, he experiences both tensions—felt by both religious and secular people. He identifies with the two groups and tries to create a framework that could include both of them and provide an answer to their points of confusion. His target audience is Israelis who want to belong to the age-old Jewish tradition—and who are proud of the fact that they are the inheritors of wisdom that has accumulated over generations—yet also want to live a life that is free of a tradition that threatens their freedom.

---

21 Michah Goodman, *The Wondering Jew: Israel and the Search for Jewish Identity* (New Haven: Yale University Press, 2020).

As an Israeli living seventy years after the foundation of the state, Goodman does not believe that secular Israeli reality is temporary and that redemption will come shortly. He accepts what those of Rabbi Herzog's generation were unable to admit, namely: that it is hard to argue that Zionism is leading history towards redemption. But for Goodman, a religious person, abandoning the vision of redemption does not undermine the validity of the Zionist project. Because he is certain about the Israeli national framework, he understands that he must change the religious justifications for Zionism. He seeks a new framework for Religious Zionism, in which Jewish content is poured into the mold of the secular national project. There is no more future to come and redemption:

> The messianists' doubts about Zionism were reinforced by a series of historic events that culminated in the 2005 Gaza Disengagement. But this skepticism is not a religious skepticism: even if the State of Israel has no messianic significance, it can still possess religious significance. Though they may not know whether the Redemption is coming, they do know that the Exile has ended, and the end of the Exile can have profound religious significance in itself.[22]

But Goodman encounters a problem. Firstly, religious Judaism requires the performance of mitzvot, not cultural commentary on secular nationalism. If Religious Zionism abandons its desire to establish a religious state, how can it grant religious justification to a Jewish state that is ruled by a secular community? He argues that halakha was created to contend with the significant fear of assimilation. Thus, halakha itself is "exilic." Judaism wanted to preserve itself, and so it put up walls. Therefore, one can tone down or even jettison some of its requirements in Israel. In any case, he argues," For the Hebrew prophets, moral sensitivity was more important than ritual exactitude."[23] To be relevant and tackle the source of its confusion, Religious Zionism must be opened up and freed from exilic, halakhic tradition in order to join the general Jewish society of Israel.

According to Goodman, connection to the national Zionist project would give freedom to religiosity, but it would also redeem secularism from the confusion of individualism. For this purpose, Israeli secularism must liberate Judaism from the hold of the Diaspora that it has clung to. Secular people can

---

22   Ibid., 111.
23   Ibid., 122.

connect to their Jewish roots in a few ways. They can create new Hebrew culture, connect forms of worship that are not centered around Jewish legal obligations, or even take ownership over the tradition and write secular "halakha" that recommends, for example, disconnecting from electronic devices on Shabbat.

Goodman attempts to sketch a new shared space that will transform religious and secular communities into one community. This shared community is, in its entirety, "Judaism." But if "halakha and belief in God no longer define the boundaries of Judaism, what does? If faith is not what connects one hundred generations of Jews, what does? The answer: "Judaism is the Jews' ongoing conversation. The conversation about Judaism is Judaism. The way Jews become connected to Judaism is by joining the Jewish conversation," Goodman answers.[24] Therefore, those who participate in conversations about Judaism take part in Judaism. It doesn't matter if they keep mitzvot and are obligated to halakha or are secular people engaged in Jewish culture.

Despite his attempt to present a Judaism that is ostensibly liberated from the traditional boundaries, Goodmanian Judaism also has boundaries, and not all can join the conversation, even if they are Jewish, or engaged with Israel. There are people on the margins of the conversation and at its center and there are people who can't take part in this conversation at all, even though the reason for their exclusion is not explicitly explained. In short, Goodman replaces one boundary of the Jewish community with another. He exchanges the covenant between God and the Jewish people, expressed through the obligation to mitzvot, for citizenship and nationalist symbols. This creates a new center and margins.

One group at the margins of this conversation is Jews who don't live in Israel. Goodman argues that Diaspora Jewish communities are either stuck in restrictive halakhic discourse or must face the danger of assimilation. Although he accepts the Judaism of this group, he maintains that it is obsolete and not meaningful for Judaism's renewal. If that is the case, it is possible to sharpen Goodman's perspective on Judaism's boundaries. It is possible to say that the conversation about Judaism is Judaism, but the discussion in Israel is preferable to that of the Diaspora.

In Israel, too, not everyone is part of his conversation. To be part of Jewish discourse about Judaism is not enough to be part of the conversation. One needs to be a Jew. It sometimes seems that Goodman speaks about all of the state's citizens as the creators of discourse on Judaism, but not all the state residents are Jews. A population group that is not mentioned even once in Goodman's

---

24 Ibid., 91.

books about the place of Judaism and the political situation is Arabs in Israel, who are about a fifth of the population. Arabs who live in Israel are citizens of the state and should be part of the conversation about Judaism in the state. If "the conversation about Judaism is Judaism," which can also be expressed through involvement in state life, then shouldn't Arab citizens of Israel can be considered "Jews," in the sense that they are involved citizens in a Jewish state? Yet Goodman ignores this population.

As we continue reading, we learn that there are different levels of belonging even within Jewish discourse in Israel. Unlike Arab citizens of Israel, ultra-Orthodox thought is mentioned in the book. Goodman identifies ultra-Orthodox thinkers as characters outside of the discourse because they do not accept the fundamental assumptions that Goodman draws upon. The ultra-Orthodox do not accept that a Jew is someone who is part of a conversation on Judaism. They do not feel confused because of their obligation to halakha, and they certainly do not see secular Israelis as part of the conversation about Judaism's renewal. Secular, atheistic communities that have no interest in being part of Jewish national discourse are also marginal for Goodman's, as is the extreme religious right that is unwilling to be in conversation with Israeli Jewish liberals. So too are Reform and Conservative Jews, which Goodman deems as marginal to the conversation. He writes:

> Let me clarify here what this book is not about: it is not about non-Israeli forms of Judaism. This is why it contains no systematic discussion of ultra-Orthodox Judaism, which has certainly evolved inside Israel but was born and developed outside Israel and cannot be considered a uniquely Israeli innovation. Neither is this book about Reform and Conservative Judaism, or other progressive streams, simply because they are not predominantly Israeli. This book is about Israeli Judaism and will advance the argument that such a phenomenon exists. Modern Israel is not only somewhere Jews live, a country like any other; it is also the soil in which a new and distinct kind of Judaism has grown. Israeli Judaism largely has two aspects, one religious, the other secular. In this section I explore the secular side of the coin: secular Zionism. Later I shall look at its twin: religious Zionism.[25]

---

25 Ibid., 43–44.

It is a problematic argument: Goodman "opens" the conversation by suggesting that "the conversation about Judaism is Judaism," but then pushes millions out of the conversation by suggesting that their Judaism (or "Israelism") is irrelevant. Perhaps rather than saying that "Judaism is the conversation about Judaism," it is more accurate to say that there are several different conversations about Judaism, and every conversation judges and undermines the assumptions of the other. Goodman's Judaism is one component of Jewish discourse. It's a discourse on Judaism in Israel, by hegemonic Zionists. It does not include those who are not Jewish and live in Israel, nor does it include Jews in Israel who oppose the renewal of Judaism in Israel or Jews who live in the Diaspora. Goodman's apparently clear, simple statement is, in fact, very complicated.

If, in any case, we want to simplify the equation, we can say that Goodman's Judaism is a conversation about modern ethnic nationalism, its symbols, and what it means to feel a sense of belonging or loyalty to Israel. True, its boundaries are not the rigid walls of halakha. But those walls are exchanged for rigid walls of national commitment to the state. Judaism, according to Goodman, is the conversation of Zionists about Judaism. Like those of the "when we are in power" school, Goodman, who does not see Torah and mitzvot as the organizing principle of the Jewish community, also distances himself from traditional religiosity, and he is also a clear product of Religious Zionism. His loyalty is not to the tradition but an ethnic state.

The two positions discussed here—the brutes of sovereignty on the Temple Mount and the renewers of Israeli Judaism—both grant types of religious value to the state. The tradition is a tool used to sanctify the secular state for both of them. The logic of Religious Zionism, which tried to subjugate the state to a religious vision, has changed. Today, religion serves the state and is subservient to it. But I do not want to surrender to the logic of the state. I want to investigate a different path: obligation to the traditional world of the rabbis within the new nation-state of the Jewish people. I want to surrender myself to religious logic from within the state I live.

4

Devotion

It is fitting for a person to resemble his Creator, for then he will be [made] in the secret of the Highest Form, in image and likeness. For if he should resemble [his Creator] in his body but not in his actions, he disappoints the Form, and they will say of him, "his form is lovely, but his deeds are ugly." For the essence of the Highest Image and Likeness is in His actions. And what benefit is it to him to resemble the Highest Form in the physical form of his limbs when his actions do not resemble those of his Creator?

—Rabbi Moshe Kordovero, *Tomer Devorah* (Safed, sixteenth century)[1]

The Question of the Traditional Jew

Being a traditional Jew means living one's life according to rabbinic tradition and belonging to communities that see themselves as obligated to the interpretive tradition of our sages and commentators. I am a traditional Jew, devoted to an Orthodox religious community.[2] I am also an Israeli, and I want to be Israeli. I am not prepared to compromise on any of my commitments. But how do I live a traditional Jewish life in this particular place and at this specific time? How does a traditional Jew live in Israel's secular, messianic state? Is it possible to be faithful to our tradition in Israel, where, too often, tradition is subordinated to state interests?

---

1 Moses Cordoyero, *Tomer Devorah*, ch. 1.
2 On the relation between loyalty and tradition, see Meir Buzaglo, *Safah la-ne'emanim: maḥshavot 'al ha-masoret* (Jerusalem: Keter, 2008), 20–27.

"You shall be holy, for I, the Lord Your God, am holy"

The midrash in Sifre Deuteronomy (chapter 49) explains:

> "to walk in all of God's ways"—what are the ways of the
> Holy Blessed One? For it states [Exodus 34], "The Lord, the
> Lord, God who is compassionate and graceful, slow to anger,
> abounding in kindness and faithfulness, extending kindness to
> the thousandth generation, forgiving iniquity, transgression,
> and sin and cleansing." And it states [Joel 3], "All who call upon
> the name of God shall escape." How is it possible for a person
> to be called by the name of the Holy Blessed One? Thus, just
> as God is called "compassionate and graceful," you should be
> compassionate and graceful and give freely to all. Just as the
> Holy Blessed One is called righteous, as it states [Psalms 145],
> "Righteous is God in all of God's ways and pious in all actions," so
> should you be righteous. The Holy Blessed One is called pious,
> as it states "pious in all actions," so should you be pious. Thus
> it says, "all who call upon the name of God shall escape." And
> it is written [Isaiah 43], "Everyone who is called by my name, I
> have created, formed, and fashioned for my honor." And it states
> [Proverbs 16], "God has created everything for a purpose."

The rabbinic midrash explains that we must imitate God by walking in God's
way. We must be compassionate in the same way that God is merciful and pious
in the same way that God is pious.

We are in dialogue with a God we cannot see, whose actions are hidden
from us. But it is by imitating God that we can get closer to God. Imagining
God's behavior towards us is a way of seeking out God's closeness. Even though
we will never be able to understand God, we still try to act like God out of a
desire both to be heard by and to give voice to God. Imitating God is itself a
constant conversation with God.

Imitating God plays an essential role in my life as a traditional Jew. The
most striking example of this is the observance of Shabbat. We keep the
Sabbath because God ceased all labor on the seventh day, as it states in Exodus
31, "the children of Israel shall keep the sabbath [...] because in six days God
made heaven and earth, and on the seventh day, God ceased from work and
was refreshed." There are many examples in the Torah of commandments to
imitate God—Deuteronomy 28:9 states, "you shall keep the commandments

of the Lord your God and walk in God's ways" and Leviticus 19:2 states, "speak to the whole Israelite community and say to them, 'you shall be holy, for I, the Lord your God, am holy.'" The rabbis and the later commentators who came after them expanded the idea of imitating God's actions to include adopting God's good attributes as well. Thus, we learn in the Babylonian Talmud (Sotah 14a):

> Rabbi Hama, son of Rabbi Hanina, said, What does it mean [Deuteronomy 13:5] "you shall walk after the Lord your God?" Is it possible for a person to walk after the Divine Presence? It has already been stated [Deuteronomy 4:24] "For the Lord, your God is a devouring fire! Rather, this means that one must follow the attributes of the Holy Blessed One. Just as God clothes the naked, as written [Genesis 3:21], "the Lord God made garments of skin for Adam and his wife and clothed them," so too should you clothe the naked. Just as the Holy Blessed One visits the sick, as it is written [Genesis 18:1]. "God appeared to him by the terebinths of Mamre," so too should you visit the sick. Just as the Holy Blessed One comforts mourners, as it is written [Genesis 25:11], "it was after the death of Abraham and God blessed his son Isaac," so too should you comfort mourners. Just as the Holy Blessed One buries the dead, as it is written [Deuteronomy 34:6], "and buried him in the valley, so too should you bury the dead.

God's Daily Schedule

A famous story (midrash) in the Talmud, in the tractate of Avodah Zara, describes God's daily routine. Understanding this schedule can help us orient how traditional Jews could behave in the world, that is, act responsibly towards both the community and the wider world. In the story's description of God's daily schedule, I have found an orientation and possible answer to the question of traditionalism in a time of Jewish power. Perhaps this tale can point us towards the beginning of a broader response to the challenges facing traditional Jews in Israel today. This answer is both ethical and political, and can be an invitation to conversation about our tradition from a place of shared, collective desire to create a traditional Jewish way of life in Israel.

> Rav Yehuda says that Rav says: There are twelve hours in the day.
> During the first three hours, God sits and engages in Torah study.
> God sits and judges the whole world in the second set of hours.
> Once God sees that the whole world is liable for destruction,
> God rises from the throne of judgment and sits on the throne of
> mercy. In the third set of hours, God sits and sustains the entire
> world, from the horns of oxen to lice eggs. In the fourth set of
> hours, God sits and plays with the Leviathan, as it says, '"there is
> the leviathan, whom you formed to play with."
> —Avodah Zara, 3b

The midrash divides God's day into four equal parts, each of which is
designated for a different area of divine activity.

The First Part of the Day: Torah Study

"In the first three hours, God sits and engages in Torah study."

What does the Master of the Universe and the Sovereign of All Deeds do
upon awaking in the morning? Learn Torah, of course—because it is impossible
to act in the world without learning Torah. There is undoubtedly an element of
irony in the fact that an omnipotent God needs to study the Torah to articulate
and be reminded of His worldview. Yet, this irony only serves to emphasize the
importance of Torah study in the life of traditional Jews. If God needs to study
Torah, how much more so must we set regular times for Torah study in order
to act in the world. Unlike certain other activities, learning Torah is not done in
isolation but is a communal activity. For one to be able to learn, there needs to
be a learner and a teacher. Even if the teacher is a book, the book was written by
another person, a present-absent teacher. The connection between the learner
and the teacher forms the basis of traditionalism, to which we are obligated and
is the core of our traditional language.

Maimonides writes in the *Laws of Torah Study*:

> Just as a person must teach his child, so too must he teach his
> child's child, as it says, "make them known to your children
> and your children's children" [Deuteronomy 4:9]. And not
> only his child and his child's child, but it is an obligation that
> every wise person in Israel teach every student, even though

they are not his children, as it says, "you shall teach your children" [Deuteronomy 6:7]—we learn from the oral tradition that "your children" refers to your students, for students are also called children, as it states 'the children of the prophets went forth' [II Kings 2:3]. [. . .] One who his parent did not teach must teach himself when he can understand, as it says, "you shall learn them, and you shall keep them to do them" (Deuteronomy 5:1). Similarly, one finds that in all cases, study precedes action because studying leads to action, but action does not lead to studying.[3]

Studying can lead to action, but for this to be the case, one must study in the context of tradition and community; otherwise, the deed is lacking. The Talmud (Brachot 47b) teaches us that "serving Torah scholars" is one of the forty-eight ways the Torah is acquired. The value of serving Torah scholars is so significant because it embodies the idea that Torah study is carried out as part of a chain of traditions. Setting regular times for Torah study is part of the very construction of our identity, which we do by engaging in our practice, regularly visiting *batei midrash* (houses of study), and learning the traditional language of Jewish texts.

Learning does not only happen within the community; it also creates community and designates its boundaries. This means that learning defines who are members of the community. The base of our community's tradition is the Jewish family—parents and children who fulfill mitzvot and study Torah together. This is both a communal unit and a political community with boundaries. These boundaries are constructed first and foremost by faithfulness to the tradition we are obligated to. Learning helps us understand the roots of devotion—the moment of divine revelation to the Jewish people on Mount Sinai and the ways to preserve and explore those exact boundaries in our daily lives. Learning Torah is not only an activity of preservation; it is also how we figure out how to integrate Torah into our lives in a way that takes seriously and is faithful both to Torah and to the reality in which we live. The learner does not only transmit information onward but creates and renews the Torah's content.

The nature of community and even of family has changed historically. In the modern era, Jews are granted far more ability to choose how they live than Jews born into communities a hundred years ago or a few dozen years ago. Despite these dramatic changes, there are still points of similarity. Even if the family has

---

3   Maimonides, *Mishneh Torah, Laws of Torah Study* 1:3, 36.

changed, the process and importance of intergenerational transmission have remained intact. Even if communities have changed, synagogues and *houses of study* have remained central anchors and obligatory institutions in traditional Jewish life.

The foundation of Jewish life, families and communities generate diverse interpretations and halakhic rulings. Debate is an integral part of the beit midrash and religious communities. For example, there is a moral debate about advancing gender equality in synagogues today. Each side relies upon the legitimacy of its halakhic interpretation and arrives at different conclusions.[4]

The community and the family institutions express and actualize tradition, playing a crucial role in determining the direction of our lives. Due to this, it would be wrong for a state to be the body regulating tradition and rituals. A state is a secular body that organizes our civic lives, while a religious community is a human society united by a cultural, legal, and religious tradition. A state must safeguard the right of communities and families to exist, but it does not have the authority to define practices or their boundaries.

State laws do not concern Jewish law, and the state is not the expression of our identity or a supreme authority to regulate our lives. Throughout the generations, Jewish tradition has recognized that there are kingdoms in the world that have power that is not religious. Traditional Jews are obligated to obey the laws of the secular authority (*Dina d'malchuta Dina*—"the law of the land is the law"),[5] as long as those laws don't require them to transgress the laws of the Torah, but, importantly, the state's laws and identity do not define the religious community.

There is no way to understand what it means to be a separate community and constantly remind ourselves of this fact without consistent engagement in the study of Torah, halakha, history, and the good attributes Torah requires of us.

---

4   See for example Daniel Sperber, *Darkah shel halakhah: ḳeri'at nashim ba-Torah: peraḳim bi-mediniyut pesiḳah* (Jerusalem: Rubin Mass, 2007).

5   See B. *Baba Batra*, 54b. Although the law of *Dina d'malchuta dina* pertained originally to the Jewish community in Babylonia, and later to Jews living under non-Jewish governments, it is claimed by some rabbis that as long as a state is not a halakhic state, the principle applies. See, for example, the responsum by Rav Ovadia Yosef, *Yeḥave Da'at*, 5:64: "See that also in a state that isn't ruled by king, but rather by a government elected the state's residents, the principle *dina d'malchuta dina* is still relevant regarding taxes, property tax, customs, etc."

The Second Part of the Day: Judgment

"In the second set of hours, God sits and judges the world. Then, once God sees that the whole world is liable for destruction, God rises from the throne of judgment and sits on the throne of mercy."

After the hours of study, which allow us to participate in tradition and create community, it is time to observe the world critically. God looks up from studying and looks around. God sees the world sinning. God is not apathetic to the sins of the world. God judges this reality, and every day at the same time, God determines the world ought to be destroyed. Yet every day, the world remains intact. God does not destroy the world, not because of a lack of ability to do so, but because after judgment, He moves to the throne of mercy and then chooses to continue maintaining the world. God does not want to destroy the world, and mercy allows God to maintain it. The next day, God will again observe the world with judgment and move to the throne of mercy.

Like God, we, too, since gathering as a community of learners, observe the world around us and judge it. While it is not within the state's power to dictate the life of traditional societies, this work is nonetheless political. It is political in another sense, in the sense of social relations—the work of guiding our communities teaches us about the correct use of power and authority. As I understand it, the Torah requires that we take a stand about what is happening in the world around us. Retreating into our community or separating ourselves from our surroundings is neither desirable nor possible. Our learning in the beit midrash is incomplete if it has no orientation towards the outside world. The Torah teaches, "you shall surely rebuke your fellow and bear no sin on his account." Maimonides explains that this verse means that "one who sees his fellow sinning or following a bad path is obligated to return him toward the good and to let him know that he is sinning against himself through his bad deeds, as it says, 'you shall surely rebuke your fellow.'"[6] Traditional Jews must have a position on everything, and this position must be formulated through an in-depth study of religious sources. This means that we are also obligated by the opinions that we form to rebuke and criticize our surroundings.

Traditional Jews must ask themselves what God wants from us, and they must, from within the beit midrash, formulate a position on the social-political reality in which the beit midrash is situated. I admit that this thought intimidates me at times. It is easy for us to think that the world of Torah is tucked into itself,

---

6   Maimonides, *Mishneh Torah, Laws of Ethical Behavior* 6:7, p. 32

that it has no opinion about what is happening around us. But that is simply untrue. We are required to formulate an ethical-religious position on every issue. We must cultivate a religious position on Israel's control of the territories and its residents, gender, problems of the environment, and matters of social justice.

One of the most critical aspects of Jewish tradition is its dynamism. People are not outside of history in traditional interpretations and understandings of the world. There is a complicated relationship of mutual influence between the community of believers and the tradition that unites them.

We see this idea, for example, in the writings of the Ḥida, Rabbi Chaim Yosef David Azulai, who lived in the eighteenth century. He wrote in "Offerings: The Laws of Reading the Torah," chapter 13 of his book *L'david Emet*:

> a Torah scroll is unpointed so that a person can interpret as desired, because the letters, when they are unpointed, tolerate several intentions and divide into several sparks, and because of this, we were commanded not to point a Torah scroll. Because the meaning of every word is according to the pointing, rather than the meaning being with the pointing, it is only of one matter, but without pointing, a person can understand several serious and wonderful matters. Understand this because you will need it in many places.[7]

So, too, Rabbi Eliahu Bachur Hazan wrote: "Because the holy Torah was given to corporeal people, who are likely to experience much change with the passing of time and eras, rulers and decrees, seasons and temperaments, states and climates—because of this, all the words of the Torah were given ambiguously within great wisdom and receive a true interpretation in every moment and at all times."[8] So, too, Ben-Zion Meir Hai Uziel wrote, "Living conditions, changes in values, and the discovery of technology and science give birth in every generation to new questions and problems which require answers. We cannot avert our gaze from these questions and say 'anything new is prohibited by the Torah,' meaning that anything not explicitly mentioned by those who came before us is considered to be prohibited."[9]

---

7   Haim Yosef David Azulai, *L'David Emet* (Livorno, Moshe Aharon Kegil, 1826), 48a.

8   Eliyahu Hazan, *Zikhron Yerushalaim* (Livorno: Eliyahu Benamozegh, 1873), 57.

9   Ben-Zion Meir Hai Uziel, "Introduction," in *Sefer Mishpetei 'Uzi'el: she'elot u-teshuvot* (Jerusalem: The Committee for Publishing the Writings of Rav Uziel, 2005), ix-x.

We can be part of the traditional chain that connects different and distant generations into one community despite how times change. However, just as we are required to be honest when we judge and assess our surroundings, we must also be frank in reading our traditions. To interpret the tradition, we must try and understand the ethical reality in which traditional texts were written. People wrote our holy books, and like us, their forms of self-expression and understanding of the Torah are inseparable from the spirit of the times in which they lived. Connecting texts and traditional values to the reality of our lives and the language of the communities we live builds traditional life.

Imagined adherence to an ahistorical understanding of the intention behind classical Jewish while remaining blind to contemporary reality and changes in historical conditions is possible, but this orientation is also an interpretive decision and is, in my opinion, a wrong one. On the contrary, it is precisely the attempt to adhere to the tradition without changes that creates new values. Moreover, any effort to implement texts literally in a changing reality requires one to be inattentive to the context in which ideas and views developed and thus narrows traditional discourse.

We saw an example of this in the previous chapter. Religious Zionism subordinated the concept of ger toshav, an idea that it reads as disconnected from its historical logic to the logic of citizenship in a nation-state. Religious Zionism interprets it as a timeless Jewish entity. But a ger toshav, to say nothing of the modern State of Israel, is not a timeless concept. Rather, it is situated within a particular historical and ethical context. To be active partners in our tradition's development, we must rely on our ethical understanding and be conscious of our place in history in attempting to interpret God's will. People who see their decisions as expressions of religious obligations and ethics will act according to religious obligations and ethical values, as each inspires an understanding of the other.

Many subsections of Religious Zionism demonstrate an understanding of the importance of historicization and change regarding specific issues. One example of this is the matter of women learning the Torah, something that Jewish tradition prohibited in the past. Today, women study Talmud in many parts of the Religious Zionist world because there is a widespread understanding that times have changed.[10] However, around the issue of our relationship to gentiles, we find a narrowing of the traditional discourse and a surprising ahistoricism. This is

---

10 For more on this topic, see Yair Etinger, *Perumim: ha-maḥloḳot she-mefatslot et ha-Tsiyonut ha-datit* (Hevel-Modi'in: Dvir, 2019), 59–80.

especially surprising because, unlike the issue of gender, the question of relating to non-Jews is significantly less unequivocal in Jewish history.

There are diverse perspectives on non-Jews in the Jewish tradition.[11] These differences are expressed in discussions of a variety of matters in Jewish texts, such as in attempts to define who and what a gentile is and debates on internal divisions and "hierarchies" within the non-Jewish world (such as between idol worshippers and non-idol worshippers), and discussions about individuals and groups of non-Jews who are worthy of imitation.[12] Similarly, the distinctiveness of Jewish identity is neither fixed nor uniform. For example, the Jewish tradition contains different understandings of the magnitude of "chosenness," ranging from perspectives on ethnic heritage to views based on the individual's voluntary choice.[13] In addition, there is also the question of the right way for a Jew to use force from a position of sovereignty. Awareness of the existence of different ethical positions shouldn't prevent us from judging and criticizing other positions, but it does mean that we must have humility regarding our position. And here we return to the midrash and God's daily schedule.

Like God, we cannot be satisfied with judgment; we also need to be compassionate. Compassion allows for tolerance that the throne of justice cannot maintain. One shouldn't confuse a firm position of discernment with trampling over every position that opposes our traditional interpretation. Like God, we cannot always act according to our judgment. There is no reason to expect that the just position will be the only position, and we must not destroy the world but rather act within it from a place of attentiveness and persuasion.

Compassion and lovingkindness complete justice. There is no meaning in understanding the Torah or the principles of the beit midrash if we do not examine reality in light of these principles, according to the value of justice. Without compassion, we would be obsessed with control and forcibly imposing our position. Therefore, as individuals and communities, we must live our lives, as reflected by an understanding of the Torah, interpreted according to the reality of our times, avoiding force and demonstrating tolerance towards both those within our communities and those outside of them.

---

11 See Ishay Rosen-Zvi, "The Birth of the Goy in Rabbinic Literature," in *Mitos, riṭu'al u-misṭikqah: meḥkarim li-khevod Prof. Itamar Grinyald*, ed. G. Bohak, Y. Rosen-Zvi, and R. Margolin (Tel Aviv: University Tel Aviv, 2014), 361–438.

12 See for example the imitation of seclusion practices of the "Muslim Dervishes" in Abraham Maimon, *Ha-Maspik le-'ovdey ha-Shem* (Jerusalem: n.p., 2019), 232.

13 See for example Hannah Kasher, 'Elyon 'al *kol ha-goyim* (*Devarim* 26 19): *tsiyune derekh ba-filosofyah ha-Yehudit be-sugyat ha-'am ha-nivḥar* (Tel Aviv: Idra, 2018).

The Third Part of the Day: Halakha

"In the third set of hours, God sits and sustains the entire world, from the horns of oxen to the eggs of lice."

After learning Torah and sitting in judgment, God begins to act in the third part of the day: God sustains the world. The transition from learning and judgment in the first half of the day to action in the second half is essential for my understanding of how to live as a traditional Jew.

In the Talmud (Kiddushin 40b), there is a famous debate between Rabbi Tarfon and Rabbi Akiva about whether learning or action is preferable. Rabbi Tarfon prefers action, and Rabbi Akiva prefers learning. The sages settle the dispute and say, "learning is great for it leads to action," meaning action is impossible without learning. This means that learning must lead to action. They are bound up with one another. The result of moving to the throne of mercy in motion is feeding the world. First, there is learning, then judgment has its turn—which means contemplating the world from a place of learning—and then action. The power that we exercise in the world is adapted to the circumstances in which we act.

When traditional Jews act, they try to act from a place of Torah learning. Torah and traditional commentaries show me how to act according to the tradition and halakha. The world of halakha and tradition surrounds me and regulates my day and my life—both personal and public. It is much more than private ritual. In my understanding, halakha is an all-encompassing legal system that touches on all areas of life. Therefore, just as God is concerned with the whole world, so too must I be concerned, and act from, a similar place of all-encompassing concern.

It is impossible to understand traditional Jewish life without understanding the place of halakha in both personal and communal life. The rabbinic enterprise created comprehensive, practical interpretations of the Torah, which organizes Jews' lives in every domain. Halakha includes many diverse areas: laws around ritual and sacrifices, family law, tort law, legal and punitive systems, and more. Indeed, there are some who claim that halakha is an inflexible system that forces itself upon people who keep mitzvot and prevent critical thinking. In the previous chapter, we saw how Goodman, in this context, wrote, "Orthodox Jews are often called on to surrender their humanistic values. Having grown up in modern societies and absorbed and internalized those societies' values, they often experience a clash between the conscience that guides them and the tradition that binds them. And their values, which they feel compelled to live by, are silenced in favor of their religion, which they feel compelled to obey."[14] In discussing issues such as the use of force, the value of equality, and the relationship with gentiles, some of my friends, including religious ones, recoil from engaging with the world of halakha. Jews who aspire to equality do not like to talk about halakha's relationship with gentiles.

However, halakha is not inflexible; instead, it is a transparent system in whose creation people are invited to participate. The halachic system is open to everyone, so halachic decisors explain why they ruled the way they did. Critique of the halachic system stems from recognizing its obligatory nature, and the knowledge that it contains problematic laws. But an in-depth look at the halachic system makes it possible to see that halakha results from both learning and taking a position and reflects diverse social, cultural, and ethical considerations, and that one can engage with problematic laws.

For me, it is critical to contend with the relationship of halakha to gentiles, primarily because of the centrality of the issue in our lives. The halachic system allows us to conduct a critical and open conversation about the relationship between Jews and gentiles. The core issues of such a conversation—endogamy, fear of the stranger, love of the neighbor, maintenance of neighborly relations, feelings of superiority and inferiority, and the use of force—are discussed in halachic texts.

One example is an issue that sometimes makes headlines in Israel—the kashrut status of restaurants that employ Arab cooks. In the spring of 2020, this issue was brought up in the context of a café in Jerusalem that lost its kashrut certification when the state mashgiach (kashrut supervisor) saw an Arab cooking an omelet in the kitchen.[15] Social media overflowed, justifiably so, with arguments about the relationship between religion and state. The fact that the state, through the chief rabbinate, discriminated against a cafe that employed a non-Jewish cook is indeed troublesome. The voices against the rabbinate called for separating religious institutions from state institutions. But for someone who keeps mitzvot, these calls are not enough. Even if a restaurant does not have kosher certification from the state, the ethical question remains about the prohibition of eating in a place where an Arab cooks.[16]

---

14 Michah Goodman, *The Wondering Jew*, 3.

15 Shlomi Heller, "Taking Away of Kosher Certificate from Kalo—Will Jerusalemites Display Solidarity," *Kol Ha'ir*, June 29, 2020, https://www.kolhair.co.il/jerusalem-news/133613/.

16 For more on this, see Ethan Tucker, "Maintaining Jewish Distinctiveness: The Case for Gentile Foods," Center for Jewish Laws and Values, accessed 22 May 2023, https://www.hadar.org/torah-resource/maintaining-jewish-distinctiveness-case-gentile-foods.

As I have explained, I think we should grapple with halakha—not ignore it or treat it as a purely formalistic system. In this case, we can start from a responsum of Rabbi Ovadia Yosef in his book of responsa *Yechaveh Data*. This is the question asked of the rabbi:

> Hotels and restaurants that have a kashrut supervisor from the local chief rabbinate and have kashrut certification, although the cook who cooks the dishes in these places is an Arab, the cooking and baking ovens are lit by a Jew who is the kashrut supervisor, is it permitted to eat these dishes, without fear of violating the prohibition on eating food cooked by gentiles?[17]

The anonymous questioner knows that *bishul goy* (food cooked by a gentile) is prohibited but wonders whether in Israel, in a case where an Arab works for a Jew, the situation is different. This social instinct is essential. The questioner identifies the change in social reality as an opening to ask anew about the appropriate relationship to this prohibition.

Rav Ovadia surveys the different halachic views that have developed around the question of food cooked by a gentile describes the prohibition as it is discussed in the Talmud (Avodah Zara, in a text related to concerns around idol worship), and demonstrates how a particular logic of separation developed in halachic texts. One reason given in halachic texts why food cooked by a gentile is prohibited is because of a fear that a gentile cooking food for a Jew does not know the laws of kashrut. Another reason is a fear of social mixing that could lead to intermarriage, referred to in rabbinic and halachic literature as *mishum chestnut*. Finally, the desire for separation between Jews and gentiles sprung from a lack of trust and a fear of erasing the boundaries between communities.[18]

The traditional logic tries to preserve the community and therefore does not see a separation between Jews and gentiles as an ethical problem. More so, when we follow the historical development of this issue, we learn that halachic authorities connected separateness and power. Thus we learn that many halachic decisors ruled that when in a Jew's own home or when a Jew is in charge, there is less of a halachic problem with food cooked by a gentile. Food cooked by a gentile is only problematic when Jews are in a weak and vulnerable

---

17 Rav Ovadia Yosef, *Yeḥave Da'at*, 5:54.
18 For more on the development of these concepts, and a critique of the assumption that the rabbis saw in gentile cooking something with prevents kashrut, see Zvi Aryeh Steinfeld, "The Meaning of the Prohibition of Gentile Cooking," in 'Am *le-vadad: meḥkarim be-Masekhet* 'Avodah *zarah* (Ramat-Gan: Bar-Ilan University, 2008), 149–165.

relationship with non-Jews because there is a greater fear of the community's disintegration.

Halachic traditions developed following different conditions and changing power relations between Jews and gentiles.[19] The tradition that gives significant weight to power relations between Jews and non-Jews developed in Europe and not in the halachic tradition that Rav Ovadia belongs to.

As we have seen, halakha contends with an abundance of social and historical positions and rules under changing realities. After surveying the halachic history, Rav Ovadia presents the stringent Sephardi position, meaning the position that sees fear of gentiles—a fear that is not dependent on power relations—as its starting point. However, despite this, Rav Ovadia notes that the prohibition on eating food cooked by a gentile is not unequivocal. And in truth, many Mizrahim follow Rav Ovadia's ruling and stay at hotels and eat at restaurants in which non-Jews cook, even though this was not the stringent Sephardic ruling in the Diaspora. In other words, Rav Ovadia goes out of his way to be lenient and even rules against the strand in traditional halachic rulings that he is generally committed to—all for social-ethical reasons. In a reality in which Jews are strong and less vulnerable, there is less fear of losing communal identity.

Despite what we have discussed above, halachic logic is not universalist; it does seek to absolve Jewish particularity. Even if halakha permits interreligious social mixing in a context of sovereignty and power, it does so because the system doesn't fear the collapse of distinctiveness in such a situation.

Indeed, those whose moral language opposes any practical expression of distinctiveness will not find their home in the halachic world (and one can assume that they will also not find their home in the language of modern nationalism). Halachah is premised upon the idea that in "this world," there are different communities and different cultures, and one should preserve the traditional communal structure. Separation is intended to protect the culture and tradition of Jews who are weak. In today's Israel, Jews are strong, not helpless. To deny this change and to read halakha as if we were still weak and vulnerable is a denial of reality and, therefore, a distortion of halachic logic.

Nevertheless, is it possible to imagine a world without boundaries between "us" and "them"? This question brings us to the final portion of God's day.

---

19 This way of thinking developed especially among European rabbis, and is mentioned by Rav Ovadia Yosef. See note 17 above.

The Fourth Part of the Day: Power

"In the fourth set of hours, God sits and plays with the leviathan, as it says [Psalms 104], 'there is the leviathan, whom you formed to play with.' Rav Nahman bar Yitzhak said: 75."

The Leviathan is mentioned several times in Jewish texts, always negatively. Several rabbinic midrashim teach us about the Leviathan and its tremendous power. In Bava Batra 75, it states, "When the leviathan is hungry, it produces breath from its mouth and boils all of the waters in the depths of the sea." The Talmud also tells of

> Rabbi Eliezer and Rabbi Yehoshua who were traveling on a ship, and Rabbi Eliezer was sleeping, and Rabbi Yehoshua was awake. Rabbi Yehoshua trembled, and Rabbi Eliezer awakened. Rabbi Eliezer said to him, "what is this, Yehoshua? Why did you tremble?" He answered, "I saw a great light in the sea." Rabbi Eliezer replied, "Perhaps you saw the eyes of the leviathan, as it is written [Job 41:10] 'and its eyes are like the eyelids of dawn.'"

The Leviathan is a monster of tremendous strength whose power is destructive and murderous. The Leviathan is not a god or of a different belief system. Nevertheless, the it is scary, and its power is tremendous. Its eyes can blind, its stench can kill, and it voraciously devours other sea creatures. Human beings cannot control the creature; it is a product of God's handiwork. The midrash tells us that God created the Leviathan as both male and female but, fearing that they would increase, He killed the females. Even God needed to restrain its tremendous power, and only God could control it. There is a long textual history to the monster, but it is always identified with power throughout this history. It is most well-known in the modern era because of the work of the philosopher Thomas Hobbes, whose book *Leviathan* describes the political power of the sovereign, who rules over his subjects and embodies the state in his body.

The philosopher Simone Weil wrote in her essay "The Iliad, or, The Poem of Force": "To define force—it is that x that turns anybody who is subjected to it into a thing. Exercised to the limit, it turns a man into a thing in the most literal sense: it makes a corpse out of him. Somebody was here, and the next minute there is nobody here at all."[20] Weil surveys the meanings of the destruc-

---

20 Simone Weil, "The Iliad, or the Poem of Force," *in War and the Illiad*, trans. Mary McCarthy (New York: New York Review of Books, 2005), 3.

tive force outside of our control, and she argues that anyone who uses force will eventually be defeated by it. Power blinds and gives one a false feeling of ownership over it. However, reality will always overcome those who believe that they control power rather than power controlling them. In our rabbinic tradition, one can imagine that Weil's "force" is the Leviathan. The Leviathan is human strength and physical force. It is external to us and stronger than us. Therefore, it cannot be truly controlled.

Force is God's handiwork, not our own, and before entering the Land of Canaan, the Children of Israel are warned not to forget this fact. Deuteronomy 8, God says,

> Your herds and flocks have multiplied, your silver and gold have multiplied, and everything you have has increased. Your heart will grow haughty, and you will forget the Lord your God who brought you out of the land of Egypt, the house of bondage, who led you through the great and terrible desert, with its scorpions and snakes, a parched land with no water in it, who extracted water for you from the rocks of flint, who fed you manna in the desert which your ancestors did not know, to test you by hardships to benefit you in the end. And you will say in your heart, 'my own power and the might of my hands made this wealth for me.

Whether in one's heart or publicly, the statement that power and strength are our stands opposes Jewish tradition.

However, despite the Leviathan's power and its negative depiction in rabbinic sources, we discover in our midrash that God plays with the same Leviathan in the fourth part of the day. The Creator of the entire universe plays with power. How is this possible? The midrash sketches a new timeline around the nature of power and its use.

The continuation of the section in the Talmud shows that the rabbis understood the problem. How is it possible, the Gemara asks, that God plays with the Leviathan after the destruction of the Temple? God does not play in this world with leviathans. The destruction of the Temple and the exile of God's presence upset the balance of the world, allowing for joy and play around with corporeal power. The Talmud answers, indeed, it is so. God does not play with the Leviathan in this world. The heavenly balance between divine power belongs to a different world, a world before the destruction of the Temple, when God's real physical presence was active in our world. After the destruction of the Temple, God exchanged the last part of the daily schedule with another activity, teaching the children of the schoolhouse: "In the fourth set of hours, what does God do? God sits and teaches the children of the schoolhouse Torah, as it says [Isaiah 28:9], 'To whom does God teach knowledge, and to whom does God make understand the message? To those just weaned off milk, just drawn away from the breast.'" This world is a world in which the power of the Leviathan is not still one of play. The balance between God and the Leviathan was breached, and it's no longer possible to benefit from its power. Today we are in the present, in this age, where the Leviathan is purely negative—a destructive power which, even if it is part of the world and even if it is necessary, will ultimately lead to devastation.

Interestingly, the future is not a return to the balance between power and divinity. On the contrary, when the rift of the destruction of the Temple occurred, a new understanding came into being. As it says in the Babylonian Talmud (Bava Batra 75a), "in the future, God will make a feast for the righteous from the Leviathan's flesh."

It is hard for me to imagine a world without power. But my inability to paint a mental picture need not prevent me from developing an ethical-religious approach that strives towards such a goal, just like I imitate God even though I cannot know God's particularities. My aspiration toward a world without force leads me to recoil from and disagree with using power in the present. While disciples of nationalism imagine a return to a world that was lost, we can imagine a future that is like nothing that has ever come before it. Victory does not mean control over power but instead means living life in a world that doesn't have power, that doesn't have the Leviathan. The prophet Isaiah, in a chapter in which he offers consolation by describing the future (chapter 27), says, "On that day, God will punish the Leviathan with God's great, mighty, and strong sword." In the prayers on Hoshana Rabba at the end of the holiday of Sukkot, we pray for a future in which the righteous will dwell in a sukkah made from the skin of the Leviathan. In the grace after meals for Sukkot, there is a custom to say, "May the Merciful One allow us to merit to sit in the sukkah of the leviathan's skin." It is impossible to prevail over the power of the Leviathan in war; it is only possible to overcome through the performance of mitzvot because any use of physical force is a capitulation to the Leviathan itself.

In Yalkut Shimoni, a collection of early midrashim that was printed in the sixteenth century, a midrash states: "Whoever performs the mitzvah of sukkah in this world, God will seat them in the sukkah of the leviathan in the future." Power, the Leviathan, will die in the future.

In the meantime, we are in this world. We cannot pretend that power doesn't exist, or that force isn't sometimes a necessity. But we must reflect on the place of power in our world, even when this power serves us. Just like God no longer views power as something suitable to play with yet created the Leviathan, we must also look at power from the Jewish perspective that it requires—with doubt. Power is outside of us, sometimes necessary but always harmful. The fact that we have power does not mean that we rule over it. On the contrary, we must always be suspicious of it.

In the seventy years following the horrors of the Holocaust, in which one-third of the Jewish people and the vast majority of traditional Eastern European Judaism were destroyed, Jews have amassed significant power. This power has created a new reality: we are still living in an era when God's face is concealed from us following such destruction, but we can now imagine that because our power is so tremendous, it is somehow something positive, something that we need not hesitate in using.

The power of the Leviathan is not another form of force external to the traditional Jewish world; it is the power of Jewish society in Israel, of which traditional Jews are part. Thus the tremendous power of the Leviathan is no longer an external threat but rather an internal threat. Our engagement with national power is an engagement with power that is in our hands. I am not proposing that we deny the existence of power, but instead, I aim to cast doubt on the justifications for its use. We must be skeptical when confronting the feeling that we are the masters of our strength, and we must use it only in the absence of other choices; and we must certainly not think that the very fact of using force is a religious act.

We live within a Zionist framework and are part of its central project. We speak in its language, pay taxes to its institutions, and send our children to its schools. This is not purely a formal kind of belonging but an actual identification. This participation involves solidarity and shared hopes and fears. But how traditional Jews justify using power must be based on a value system that understands that any power is not our own. Therefore, even when there is a Zionist, nationalist justification for the use of force, traditional Jews must ask themselves if we, as individuals and as a community of believers, are allowed to use this power. Every action that the nation state takes requires believers to ask an additional question, which deviates from the assumptions of the state: Do I, as a traditional Jew, need to participate in this action? Participation in the Zionist project creates an affinity between Jews in Israel (and around the world), but the sense of belonging to a traditional community of believers creates a feeling of distance from this project—the distance from the flaunting of power, distance from the feeling of ownership over it, and distance from justifying the use of force simply because we can.

5

Contentment

As for ethical training, which means training the soul to achieve inner humility in accordance with the aggressiveness of pride and taking the form of extreme humility, this entails staying away from authority and arrogance, and abandoning jealousy and strife . . . and dwelling in magnificent palaces, and distancing oneself from prideful people . . . and by accustoming one's soul to forgive those who have done one.

—Avraham Ben HaRambam, *Hamaspik L'Ovdei Hashem*
(Egypt, thirteenth century)[1]

Every state engages with difficult questions regarding violence and the use of force, but these questions carry particular weight in Israel. We Israelis forcibly rule over millions of Palestinians against their wills. It has become increasingly clear that our military occupation over the Palestinians is not temporary; it has lasted for over half a century, and its end is nowhere in sight. As long as the occupation endures, we will continue oppressing millions and destroying the collective identity of an entire people. As the occupation becomes more firmly entrenched, we consider it an essential part of being an Israeli: any opposition to the occupation is seen as opposition to Israel's existence, and any mention of Palestinian suffering is seen as treasonous.

Religious people in Israel are especially active in advancing, maintaining, and justifying the occupation. As we saw in earlier chapters, the Religious Zionist establishment seemingly provides a stamp of approval for every Israeli military action. Moreover, Religious Zionist leaders call on the Israeli military to act with even greater aggression. And while the ultra-Orthodox consider themselves indifferent to the occupation and national issues as a whole, in reality, they constitute about 30% of all settlers. Like all settlements, Haredi settlements depend upon land theft and the oppression of nearby Palestinian

---

1   Maimon, *Ha-Maspik le-'Ovdey ha-Shem, Gate of Humility.*

communities.[2] The construction of Modiin Illit, Beitar Illit, Kochav Yaakov, Immanuel, and other settlements whose populations are primarily Haredi dispossessed thousands of Palestinians of both their livelihoods and their land.

The religious community is so prominent in the settlement enterprise and so supportive of aggressive military action that it often seems as if the natural religious position requires approval of such activities. Yet rabbinic tradition presents a very different approach to violence. To my understanding, the occupation carried out by the State of Israel is in fact halachically impermissible. Religious Jews are commanded to resist it.

"God said to me: you will not build a house to My name, for you are a man of war"

Saving a life supersedes almost every commandment in the Torah: if Jews are attacked, they must protect themselves, even if doing so means desecrating the Sabbath. War is a part of our reality in this earthly world, and people have a right, and even an obligation, to protect themselves. In the Babylonian Talmud (Eiruvin 45a), we learn:

> It is taught: if gentiles besieged a Jewish town, the Jewish residents may not go out against the gentiles with their weapons, nor may the Jews desecrate Shabbat because of the gentiles. In what case does this ruling apply? For example, when gentiles came for monetary gain, but if they came to take lives, it is permissible to go out against them with weapons and desecrate Shabbat because of them. And in a city that is close to the border, even if the gentiles came only for straw and hay, it is permissible to go out against them with weapons and desecrate Shabbat because of them.

Jews fought to preserve their own Jewish communities long before the Zionist Revolution. They also fought in larger armies. Jews, including religious Jews, served as soldiers in Prussia, France, Turkey, Iraq, England, and Germany.[3] In some of these countries, they even achieved high military rank. In Russia, over a million and a half Jews served in the army in the nineteenth

---

2   Lee Cahaner, "Between Ghetto-Politics and Geo-Politics: The Haredi Settlements in the West Bank," *Te'oryah u-vikoret* 47 (2016): 65–87.

3   Derek Penslar, *Jews and the Military: A History* (Princeton: Princeton University Press, 2013).

and twentieth centuries.[4] Many of these Jews were forcibly drafted against their will, yet certainly not all. Both those who fought willingly and were conscripted against their will received rabbinic permission to fight, to endanger themselves, and to kill.

Jewish tradition, however, recoils from the use of force. In Exodus 20:21, we are commanded: "If you make Me an altar of stones, do not build it of hewn stones; for you have profaned it by using your sword upon it." The Torah commands us to so completely distance our worship of God from the instruments of war that metal, which is used to kill human beings, cannot be used to construct the altar. To this day, according to most Jewish authorities, it is forbidden to write Torah scrolls, mezuzot, and tefillin with a quill made of metal.[5] Similarly, King David was not allowed to build the Temple because of his violent military past. "God said to me: you will not build a house to My name, for you are a man of war, and you have spilled blood" (1 Chronicles 28:3).

Rabbinic stories teach us that learning Torah, rather than physical strength, is what protects us. For example, in the Babylonian Talmud (Makkot 10a), it states: "Rabbi Yehoshua ben Levi said: What is the meaning of the verse [Psalms 122] 'Our feet were standing in your gates, Jerusalem'? What caused our feet to withstand war? The gates of Jerusalem, where they engaged in Torah study." So too, in a story in the book Vayikra Rabbah (Behukotai 35), we learn: "It was taught in the name of Rabbi Elazar: the book and the sword were given bound up together from heaven. The Holy Blessed One said to them: if you keep what is written in this book, you will be saved from the sword. And if not—in the end, it will kill you."

On the one hand, Jewish law permits, and sometimes even obligates, Jews to defend themselves, even if doing so necessitates violating other commandments. Yet violence is always considered a negative and even an abhorrent, non-Jewish trait from which one must distance oneself. While sometimes necessary, the tradition is unequivocal that Jews must always be suspicious of the use of violence.

Leaving Our Vineyard: Modern War as Tragic Necessity

The attempt to strike a balance between the permissibility of self-defense and an aversion to violence has shaped much rabbinic writing. A clear example of this

---

4   Ibid., 27-35.
5   See for example Yehiel Mekhel Epstein, Aruch ha-Shulḥan, Y. D. 271:38 (Jerusalem: Vagshal Press, 1985), 144.

balancing act is *Mahane Yisrael*, written by Rabbi Yisrael Meir HaKohen Kagan from Radun, more commonly known by the name "Chafetz Chaim."[6] Today, the Chafetz Chaim's writings can be found in diverse religious homes; Jews from Eastern European descent and Middle Eastern descent, Religious Zionists and ultra-Orthodox Jews all study his works. His *Mishnah Berura* is one of the most read halachic works of the last generations. The text, which is designed as a commentary on earlier and legal codes, summarizes and organizes the laws surrounding the daily behavior of Jews in all moments of their lives. *Shmirat HaLashon*, which discusses the laws of slander and gossip, is no less influential. For religious Jews, these books are absolute treasures. But the Chafetz Chaim also wrote many other works, including a guidebook for soldiers titled *Mahane Yisrael*.

Written in 1881, *Mahane Yisrael* was the first Jewish book intended for soldiers. The Chafetz Chaim lived in Russia, and the book's introduction focuses on military service in the czar's army, but the book could have been written for any Jewish soldier in any army in the world. The first section is comprised of halachic responsa about daily matters: prayer, ritual handwashing, the obligation to study Torah and the duty to encourage other Jews to study; the importance of keeping a kosher diet, how one repents, and how one keeps the Sabbath and Passover. The second part focuses on ethics and Jewish thought: how a soldier ought to behave with his military comrades and a prayer for peace and the redemption of the Jewish people. The work also includes a prayer that the Chafetz Chaim wrote for a soldier going out to battle. Based on the text of the confession of sins recited on the High Holidays, the prayer includes a request for divine forgiveness before going to war.[7]

The book was widely read at the time it was published, and the Chafetz Chaim remains popular today. Yet even as there is an obvious need for halachic guides for soldiers, *Mahane Yisrael* can no longer be found in bookshops or yeshivas. The only way to access it today is within a set of the entire compiled works of the Chafetz Chaim. So why has such an important book been forgotten?

The reason is its staunchly antiwar orientation. The Chafetz Chaim was no pacifist, nor did he call on Jewish soldiers to refuse military service. But he did believe that war is terrible, especially for soldiers. He writes about war as a human tragedy, not a source of human pride.[8] At the beginning of the book, he states, "From what is known to us, soldiers need God's mercy more than anyone

---

6   Yisrael Meir HaCohen Kagan, *Maḥaneh Yisrael* (Vilna: Eliezer Lipman, 1881).
7   Ibid., 95–98.
8   This opinion was not uncommon, and appeared in many rabbinic responsa in the nineteenth century. For further reading, see Judith Bleich, "Military Service: Ambivalence and

else, such as at the time of war and many other similar times."[9] The soldier here is not a hero but helpless, dependent upon God's mercy.

Within traditional Judaism, a Jew merits God's mercy by building religious and communal life. War breaks the daily patterns required for ongoing ritual and community. For this reason, Chafetz Chaim prevailed upon readers to maintain regular Jewish practice amidst the chaos of war:

> Above all else, soldiers must accustom themselves to regular mitzvot, such as saying Shema, praying, laying tefillin, and taking care to never miss these mitzvot, because in addition to the fact that they are of great holiness, as we will discuss below, another benefit [of performing them regularly as soldiers] is that after leaving the military, these mitzvot will not feel new. [10]

The life of a religious person takes place within a religious community. Jews might find themselves in the military, outside of their regular world. When religious people find themselves in such a situation, the Chafetz Chaim counsels, they should surround themselves with God, who will protect them physically and spiritually and serve as an anchor connecting them back to the world of the Torah.

"To what is the matter similar?," the Chafetz Chaim asks:

> To a person who, for whatever reason, must leave his vineyard and fruit trees and guard other vineyards. Certainly, when he has free time, he will go and check on his own vineyard and add new plants to it and preserve the fruit that has already ripened." Returning to the vineyard at every possible moment is not a desertion of the army but rather how Jewish soldiers protect themselves spiritually and physically when fighting in a war. "As it states in the midrash, 'the voice is the voice of Jacob': as long as Jacob's voice can be heard in synagogues and houses of study, Esau's hands will not rule over him.

To the Chafetz Chaim, military service is not a noble service nor an opportunity to demonstrate physical force. "A soldier must be conscientious

---

Contradiction," in War and Peace in the Jewish Tradition, ed. Joel Wolowelsy and Lawrence H Schiffman (New York: Yeshiva University Press, 2007,) 415–447.

9   Kagan, Maḥaneh Yisrael, 13.

10 Ibid.

when going to war not to think, 'What heroes are we; valorous men of war,' but rather should place his refuge in God and trust God because God will help us, as it says, 'God does not desire the strength of horses nor human muscle. God desires those who fear and are dependent on God's faithful care.'"[11]

Some see such devotion as a form of passivity. Yet the Chafetz Chaim demands that the Jewish soldier make an active decision to live according to values that stand against those that prevail in battle. He requires Jewish soldiers to oppose the norms, values, and daily routine of military life.

The reality of a religious soldier serving in the Israeli army is very different from that of a Jewish soldier in the czar's army. It is, indeed, much easier to practice a religious lifestyle, both individually and communally, in the Israeli military.

But that ease is part of the problem. Alongside the ability to serve while adhering to Jewish commandments, it is increasingly difficult to maintain a separate religious world within the world of the Israeli military. The Jewish soldier in the Israeli army today no longer feels that he is tending two vineyards but rather a single one. The army is not the czar's army but "our" army. The two vineyards have become one. While their merger is central to Religious Zionism, it is foreign to Jewish tradition.

Justifying Religious War and Our Right to the Land: Religious Zionist Responses to the Occupation

The Laws of Military and War was one of the first books written for soldiers serving in the Israeli army. Published in the early '70s by Rabbi Shlomo Min Hahar, Yissaschar Goleman, and Yehuda Aizenberg, it is the Religious Zionist version of the Chafetz Chaim's *Mahane Yisrael*. The book covers much of the same ground, but in addition, it includes a chapter titled "Ethics and Combat." The chapter discusses the confrontation between the religious soldier and the Occupied Palestinians:

> In our service in the Israeli army, we impose our will upon the Arab inhabitants of the land and use weapons to preserve the borders of the land from those who plot against us. To carry out our work faithfully, we must clarify for ourselves the rightness and justice of our deeds because one who does not have answers

---

11 Ibid., 95.

to these questions is liable to reach conclusions that destabilize the moral foundation of the wars fought by the State of Israel. Because this moral foundation is the essence of our existence in this land and one of the Israeli army's sources of power, we must examine these matters with open eyes.

A soldier who undergoes a training period prepares himself for the possibility of war breaking out. He learns to use a gun to fight against the enemy who stands in front of him. Sometimes he might remember that the enemy standing before him has a family and a home, hope, and desires.

A soldier who serves in the territories encounters a new war and a new enemy: he shoots a terrorist and sees his mother and sister crying over his corpse; he arrests a terrorist and sees his small children chasing after their father.

A soldier who passes a refugee camp sees people living in terrible poverty, and he remembers that he or his friends live in a place that could have previously been the home of some of these refugees.

The hatred in their eyes becomes more tangible than the justice of our actions. The moral problem arises and intensifies, and he asks himself: why are they hungry and without homes, and we are satisfied? Why do we rule over them against their wills? What right do we have to use force?

These ethical questions arise only when we judge our deeds with a narrow perspective, only seeing a partial reality.

The justification for our actions in the Land of Israel, our right to impose our will on a hostile population, our right to settle in any place within the Land of Israel, our right to shoot terrorists and blow up their houses, even if there are women and children—the justification for all of this we will not find in daily life. Our right to all of this is found entirely in one idea: our right to exist as a nation and our right to the Land of Israel.[12]

The book's authors understand that a Jewish soldier, with a Jewish education, will look at the reality of occupation and immediately appreciate its tragic nature. Likewise, it is clear to these rabbis that a Jewish soldier serving in the

---

12 Shlomo Min Ha'har, Issachar Goleman, and Yehuda Aizenberg, *Dinei tsava u-milḥamah* (Jerusalem: Haskel Publishing, 1971), 205–207.

territories will see and feel real suffering. Yet, in their view, the moral judgment of the soldier who asks, "Why are we ruling over them against their will?," stems from a "narrow perspective."

The justification for military action against Palestinians, claim the book's authors, is a religious justification: "the right to the Land of Israel." This right, in their opinion, and in clear opposition to the advice of the Chafetz Chaim, overrides the conscience of individual Jews and requires them to actively ignore their education. There is something ironic that the way to "examine these matters with open eyes" entails closing our eyes to suffering. Rather that listening to their conscience or their tradition, the text requires traditional Jewish soldiers to take the state as the sole sovereign power to which we must be faithful. How have Religious Zionists arrived at such a conclusion?

Wars of God: Holy Wars Versus Regular Wars in Rabbinic Tradition

The central claim of Religious Zionist rabbis is a moral one. The Chafetz Chaim dealt with the morality of the Jewish soldier. Yet for Religious Zionist leaders, the Jewish institution of the State of Israel and the Jewish wars it fights stand above him. Jewish soldiers must give up their own discernment to be part of an institution that makes ethical decisions on their behalf. But what is a Jewish holy war?

Aside from the wars of all nations, in which Jews take part as individuals, Jewish tradition designates two categories of holy war: "obligatory wars" and "wars of choice." A careful examination of the rabbinic logic underlying both has much to teach us about the traditional Jewish relationship to the use of military force. It also demonstrates the massive moral and religious neglect that lies at the foundation of Israeli wars and their justification among Religious Zionists.

The book of Deuteronomy details the laws for "when you go to war." Fighting an obligatory war is a religious duty. The obligation to participate in such a war stems not from a government decree; instead, such a war is God's explicit command. The prime example of such a war is the war fought to conquer the Land of Israel, which Deuteronomy commands: "In the cities of those peoples whom the Lord your God is giving you as an inheritance, you may not let anybody remain alive. You must utterly destroy them—the Hittites, the Amorites, the Canaanites, the Perizzites, the Hivites, and the Jebusites—as the Lord your God has commanded you."

Most medieval Talmudic commentators omitted this commandment from their compilations of the commandments, holding that this was a historical commandment relevant only to biblical times. Hivites and Canaanites don't exist anymore, and it was clear for rabbis that the commandment to go to war referred specifically to the conquering of the land of Israel written about in the Bible.

Further, religious authorities and other commentators emphasized that only a Jewish king could command an obligatory war throughout Jewish history. A king, according to religious law, is not any Jewish ruler. A king is not "chosen by the people" or someone who happens to have taken control of the government. The king's position is a religious one. He must be appointed by the Sanhedrin (the ecclesiastical high court) and approved by a prophet (a person with whom God speaks). In other words, a king is the direct emissary of God. A Jewish king is the only one who can declare an obligatory war, for a war that such a ruler decrees is a war in which God is actively present.

In addition to the Jewish "obligatory wars," Deuteronomy also describes "wars of choice." A Jewish king is permitted to go to war to expand the state's borders or even for financial reasons. But even in the case of holy wars of choice, God's explicit approval must be granted. The Babylonian Talmud (Brachot 3b) provides an example:

> A harp hung over King David's bed, and when midnight arrived, a northern wind would come and cause the harp to play above him. He would immediately rise and study Torah until the first sign of dawn. Once dawn had arrived, the Sages of Israel entered his room. They said to him, "Our master, the king, your people Israel need sustenance." So he said to them: "They should go and sustain one another." They said to him: "A single handful of food cannot satisfy a lion, nor can a pit be filled only from rainwater." So he said to them: "Go and take up arms with the troops." They immediately went to receive advice from Ahitophel and consult with the Sanhedrin and ask the Urim and Thummim [in the bible and rabbinic tradition, these are elements of the high priest's breastplate, used to answer to reveal the word of God].

In order to secure the resources for his people, King David indeed declared a holy war of choice. But to go to war, he had to receive the approval of the ecclesial high court, and consult the high priest's breastplate. Almost paradoxically, because it is not mandatory, a war of choice requires greater involvement on God's part. Wars of choice require even greater religious oversight than wars of obligation.

There are other differences between these two types of wars. For example, every Jew must participate in an obligatory war, but exemptions are granted from wars of choice. The king must have the approval of the Urim and Tumim to go to fight in the context of a war of choice, and his subjects are not required to take part in it. In Deuteronomy (20:5-8), we learn that a recently married person, a person in financial distresses, or even someone fearful is not required to go to war.

Whether obligatory or of choice, Jewish holy wars are those in which God is an active and present agent. There are defined Jewish legal requirements surrounding religious wars: the need for Jewish king, an ecclesiastical high court, and a prophet. These requirements are not merely technical; the logic underlying them ensures that a holy war is not treated as an earthly matter. The necessity of receiving permission from religious leaders is intended to prevent a situation in which all wars are granted spiritual value.

The fact that a Jewish war requires God's presence teaches us the rabbis' understanding of the essence of military violence. Jewish religion is in necessary tension with military command. A Jewish king does not run towards battles but instead studies Torah. He does not only consult military advisors; he consults the Urim and Tumim. Military actions are carried out following God's command; they are accompanied by His revelation; and they sanctify His name. There is no offense and no defense, no just or unjust wars. Jewish war is forbidden unless divine intervention permits it.

The modern State of Israel is secular and its use of force is legitimated by international law, and not by God; despite this, Religious Zionist rabbis decided that Israeli wars are holy and religiously obligatory. Thus, for example, Rabbi Yaakov Ariel, one of the most prominent Religious Zionist halachic authorities, writes: "Faithful to the belief that the commandment to settle the Land includes occupying and defending the Land, Religious Zionism fundamentally understands military service to be a mitzvah from the Torah."[13] With this interpretation, Religious Zionists have formulated a deeply heretical understanding of Jewish war. What the rabbis and the Torah insist remain separate—the military and Jewish religious life—have been made synonymous. In order to achieve this, Religious Zionists have offered a flawed and dangerous answer to the spiritual and political question that the rabbinic teaching provokes: How can one rule that Israeli wars are holy when we have no king appointed by a prophet and no ecclesial court?

---

13 Yaakov Ariel, "Religious Zionism and Halakhah," in *Halakhah Tsiyonit: ha-mashma'uyot ha-hilkhatiyot shel ha-ribonut ha-Yehudit*, ed. Y. Stern and Y. Sheleg (Jerusalem: Israel Democracy Institute, 2017), 176.

The People Are the King. Apparently.

As we saw in chapter 3, Religious Zionism considers the State of Israel a project of Jewish religion. But to mandate a holy war, more is required. To permit a Jewish war, two problems must be solved. The first and easier challenge is the need for justification: Why must a war be fought? But the second is more difficult. In an era in which no Jewish King rules, what authority could warrant a Jewish war?

Religious Zionism responds to the first question in two ways. The first is to see all of our wars as defensive. The famous medieval legalist Maimonides holds that any defensive war is an obligatory war. In the *Laws of Kings*, in his codex, the *Mishnah Torah*, he writes: "A king should not fight other wars other than an obligatory war. What is an obligatory war? This is a war against the seven nations, a war against Amalek, and to deliver Israel from an enemy that attacks them."[14]

Another possibility, which aligns well with the beliefs of Religious Zionism, can be found in the words of another medieval authority, Nachmanides, who argues that conquering the Land of Israel is a valid justification for Jewish wars. "We were commanded to inherit the land, which the Exalted God gave to our ancestors, to Abraham, Isaac, and Jacob, and it was not left in the hands of other nations or for desolation."[15]

Religious Zionist rabbis who grant religious significance to the State of Israel see these justifications as sufficient to cast every Israeli war as an obligatory holy war. Thus, for example, Rabbi Aviner writes, "The first aspect of the obligation to join the military is that of obligatory war. The second aspect is the war of conquering the Land, that is, a war of liberation, according to Nachmanides, and a defensive war according to Maimonides."[16] As we've seen from the passages quoted in this chapter, Religious Zionist leadership consistently appeals to the Jewish ownership of the land as justification for all Jewish wars.

Yet this argument on its own does not resolve the question of authority. Who has the authority to determine the conditions that allow or require going to war in the case of an obligatory war? In the very same chapters that Maimonides writes about "delivering Israel from an enemy," he emphasizes the

---

14 Maimonides, *Mishneh Torah, Laws of Kings* 5:2, 183. While this isn't the only interpretation of Maimonides, it is widely accepted within Religious Zionism.

15 Moses Naḥmanides, *Hasaggot shel ha-Ramban, Mitzva 4 Omitted* (Constantinople: David and Shmuel Naḥmias, 1510), 93.

16 Shlomo Aviner, "The Obligation for IDF Conscription," in *Me-ḥayil el ḥayil: 'inyenei tsava* (Beit El: Hava Library, 1999), 132–142.

role of the prophet in choosing the king. "A king is appointed according to a Beit Din [religious court] of 70 elders and according to a prophet, as Joshua was appointed by our teacher Moses and his court and as Saul and David, who were appointed by Samuel of Ramah and his court."[17]

In a casual aside, Rabbi Abraham Isaac HaKohen Kook attempts to address this central difficulty of how a war can be considered obligatory in the absence of a king, prophet, and legal court. Rav Kook did not write works of halakha, but his teachings were compiled posthumously by his son, Rabbi Tzvi Yehuda Kook, as books of halachic responsa literature. One of these, *Mishpat Kohen*, contains correspondence with a rabbi named Shlomo Zalman Pines in which the two discuss the Maccabean wars. There, Rav Kook asks an anachronistic question: How did the Maccabees go to war against the Greeks without a king who declared it an obligatory religious war? He answers:

> It seems that the matter is that at a time when there is no king because the laws of the kingdom relate to the general state of the nation, these legal rights are given over to the hands of the nation as a whole. In particular, it seems that any judge who arises in Israel has the status of a king regarding certain laws of kingship and especially regarding that which has to do with protecting the general public. . . . This conjecture holds up because, regarding the matter of kingship rules, which has to do with protecting the general public, it is certain that certified judges and general leaders function in place of a king. And additional support for this matter can be found in the words of Maimonides (*Laws of the Sanhedrin* 4:13): "The Heads of the Exile in Babylonia function in place of a king and can impose their will over the Jewish people anywhere." How much more so does this apply to authorized leaders of the nation, in its land and in control of its lands, of whatever level, who were given such positions to lead the nation.[18]

In short, Rav Kook claims that in the absence of a king, a representative of the people (rather than a representative of God), is the sovereign power regarding going to holy war. It is important to note that Rav Kook wrote these words in 1917, well before the foundation of the State of Israel. Despite this

---

17 Maimonides, *Mishneh Torah, Laws of Kings* 1:3, 179.

18 Abraham Isaac Kook, *Shu"t Mishpat* Kohen (Jerusalem: Mosad Harav Kook, 1966), ch. 144.

fact, leading Religious Zionist leaders—Rabbi Goren, Rabbi Yisraeli, the Tzitz Eliezer, Rabbi Min Hahar (mentioned above), and others—rely on this interpretation to rule that Israeli wars are obligatory religious wars. With this interpretation, these rabbis assert that a secular state has the authority to declare a religiously obligatory war.[19]

But in ruling that a sovereign state replaces a king anointed by a prophet, Religious Zionism contradicts the religious and moral logic of the halachic laws of war. In requiring direct divine intervention regarding any decision to go to war, the rabbinic tradition built a system founded upon suspicion of war. This does not mean that the rabbis were pacifists, but they did not ascribe spiritual value to war that weren't approved by God directly.

Contrary to this position, Religious Zionist rabbis claim that the state of Israel represents not only the entire Jewish people, but is in fact representative of God Himself. Therefore, all of the state's wars are holy wars because the state is the state of the people, and the people—today's Jewish king—are anointed by God.

Granting divine standing to secular rule renders the Israeli soldier a servant of secular nationalism. Viewing government decisions as an expression of God's will subordinates God to the will of a political ruler and prevents the religious person from discerning this will. As a result, religious soldiers are commanded to nullify their intellectual and ethical perspective and simply serve the will of a secular government. The problem is not, as is often thought, that religious values are causing harm to the secular state. The problem is that the sanctification of secularism corrupts religion and subjugates it to the changing needs of the state.

In the lead-up to Operation Pillar of Defense, for example, Givati Brigade commander and Religious Zionist Colonel Ofer Winter wrote a letter to his soldiers laden with religious language, angering many Israelis. In the letter, Winter calls upon his soldiers to fight "the terrorist 'Gazan' enemy, which abuses, taunts, and curses the God of Israel's battles." At the end of the letter, Winter declares,

> I raise my eyes to heaven and call out with you, Hear O Israel, the Lord is our God, the Lord is One. Lord, God of Israel, please, help us succeed on the path we walk and prepare to fight for the sake of your people Israel against the enemy which curses your name. In the name of IDF combatants, and especially the

---

19 See for example Stuart Cohen, "Warfare in Contemporary Jewish Law: Varieties of Analytical Frameworks," in Stern and Sheleg, *Halakhah Tsiyonit*, 186-220.

combatants of this brigade and commanding officers, fulfill what is written in the Torah, "For the Lord, your God goes with you to do battle for you against your enemies and to save you.' And let us say amen together, and only together will we achieve victory."[20]

Winter's critics argued that his religious language was unacceptable because it turned the war into a holy war. Journalists and various organizations termed Winter the head of the "Jewish Jihad Brigade."[21] Some called upon the Israeli army to dismiss him from his position. Winter's religious language, however, did not influence the brigade's military actions, and the unit acted identically to other units with secular commanders. His directive did not make the Israeli army into a religious army, change how the military operated, or create an alternate chain of command. What Winter's letter does is utilize religious language to sanctify a secular war. It uses religion to try and prevent soldiers from thinking critically about the necessity of violence or doubting the state's orders. Winter's offense was not against the state, but against Judaism.

Moshe Feinstein: An Additional Possibility for Understanding Israeli Wars

Not all Jewish legal authorities agree that wars fought by the State of Israel are obligatory religious wars. One of the most important legal authorities of the twentieth century, Rabbi Moshe Feinstein, ruled in opposition the view embraced by Rav Kook's students. In response to the question of whether the Six-Day War was an obligatory religious war, Rabbi Feinstein wrote the following letter:

> Regarding an obligatory religious war
> 25th of Tishrei 5739
> To the esteemed honor of my friend, the Rabbi, and Sage, our rabbi, and teacher, Nachum Travneck, may he live long and well, the head of the Beit Din and teacher in Kfar Chabad in the Land of Israel:

---

20 "Givati Brigade Commander: 'Studying Torah Is Best Protection,'" *Haaretz*, August 1, 2014.
21 Uri Misgav, "Israel Should Get God Out of the Army," *Haaretz*, August 8, 2014.

It is likely known to your honor that I do not hastily respond to those who ask me questions of halakha Regarding those matters about which I am not asked, it is not fitting that I should respond at all, even if it should be a particular question about the laws of kashrut. Even to those who ask me, my answers are only about individual matters that relate to the individual who asked me, and only when there was no harm to another rabbi. I have never answered a general question, neither in writing nor spoken. Maybe others have heard what I said to my students about my beliefs regarding the matter of war—that even in the name of preserving life, war requires a particular [divine] command and Urim and Tumim and the Sanhedrin, even in an obligatory religious war, such as the war against Amalek. And the necessity of [these conditions] can be seen from David and Solomon and all the righteous kings who did not fight against Amalek. This matter is straightforward, and it is not fitting to disagree. Only when the gentiles attacked the Jewish people, like Antigonus, king of Greece, and others like him, which was for defense, was there a war in the Second Temple period. I have not discussed how to decide this matter at all, not even in my own thoughts, because I shouldn't be asked about these matters by those in power in the Land of Israel. And the very case before me is irrelevant, and it is also not clear to me how to discuss it, and therefore it is not fitting for me to reply. We trust only in God, for everything is in God's hands, and we pray to God that God should have mercy upon us and upon all the Jewish people, and everything should be for good and may God send the Messiah speedily.[22]

Rabbi Feinstein's halachic logic here is the exact opposite of Rav Kook's. According to Rabbi Feinstein, no war can possibly be an obligatory holy war in the absence of a king and religious court. It is simply impossible. This does not mean that it is not permitted for Jews to wage a secular war or that the State of Israel cannot defend itself. Unlike Rav Kook, who believes that the Maccabean wars were obligatory holy wars due to the fact that in absence of king, the people represents God's will, Rabbi Feinstein says that they are simply self-defense and

---

22 Moshe Feinstein, *Iggerot Moshe, Ḥoshen Mishpat* (Bnei Brak: Feinstein, 1985), no. 78, (p. 320).

that Jews who are attacked are permitted to defend themselves, without any spiritual significance or obligation.

Regarding the Six-Day War, Rabbi Feinstein absolves himself of having to answer: "I have not discussed at all, not even in my own thoughts, how to decide this matter because I shouldn't be asked about these matters by those in power in the Land of Israel. And the very matter before me is futile."[23] Rabbi Feinstein refuses to discuss the Israeli context because he is not part of the ruling authority in Israel (that is, the Israeli government). This is a reasonable answer for a religious leader living outside of Israel. But such an answer cannot satisfy a religious Israeli citizen. Therefore, we must ask ourselves the question from which Rabbi Feinstein is exempt: If Israeli wars are not obligatory religious wars, is serving in the territories considered a secular defensive war?

No Choice?

Once it is no longer possible to utilize the concept of an obligatory religious war, justification for a religious individual to both risk themself or kill, in Israel or anywhere else in the world, would have to be self-defense. This justification would allow a religious soldier to fight, as Jewish tradition permits self-defense. Indeed, the claim of self-defense is the most often articulated secular claim in favor of the occupation.

Israelis generally view freedom as a zero-sum game: Israeli freedom, including personal and collective security, cannot exist without some control over the Palestinians. The vast majority of Israelis believe that their freedom requires the subjugation of others and that they would not be able to live freely were it not for the occupation. The Palestinian desire for their own state requires us to subjugate them. With time, this claim becomes immutable. The very idea of Palestinian freedom puts us in danger; thus, in order to win we must subjugate them.

As time passes, it becomes harder and harder for us to imagine another way of living. More and more texts are written that explains why the occupation is necessary, even if it is morally intolerable. These sorts of claims do not only come from the right. Even prominent voices in "the peace camp" aim to preserve some level of control, and significant supporters of the two-state solution call for the annexation of the Jordan Valley to control any future Palestinian borders. Moreover, almost no one supports the Palestinian right to self-defense in a

---

23 Ibid.

future state. A substantial majority of Jews in Israel insist that future Palestinian security decisions should remain under Israeli control. The internal discourse in Israeli society revolves around how much we ought to release our controlling grip over Palestinians. The idea that they would be free just like us is not even up for discussion.

It is essential to examine this position anew. Jewish tradition has much to say about secular authorities trying to convince us of false needs.

The State Knows How to Lie; the Tradition Knows How to Catch Lies

Rabbi Aharon Shmuel Tamares (1869-1931) served as the rabbi of a small community in Eastern Europe. He was known as a sharp, independent writer who sharply criticized the militarism of the Zionist movement, as well as Orthodoxy's ossification. He wrote sermons, halachic insights, and journalistic pieces, as well as personal and polemical writings.

In his book *Musar HaTorah VeHaYahadut*, a collection of his sermons for various holidays, Tamares writes about the concept of freedom. The sermon primarily deals with the appropriate relationship between war, vengeance, and violence. According to Tamares, "it is known that the purpose of the giving of the Torah was to purify people's character and to separate them from the impurity of evil deeds."[24]

Therefore, to understand the Torah, one must examine the context in which it was given: the enslavement of Israel in Egypt. The human condition on the eve of the giving of the Torah was an expression of evil.

Evil, Tamares claims, can spring from two sources. There is an evil of the body and evil of the intellect. The evil of the body, which can be understood as human or emotional evil, stems from uncontrollable human feelings—jealousy, anger, fear. All of these cause people to do wicked things, but people generally know that these are evil deeds and are ashamed of them. When people murder, steal or lie, they are typically ashamed of doing so.

The evil of the intellect, on the other hand, masks itself as a good or necessary deed. At the base of such wickedness is a lie. "Intellectual evil, deceptive evil, political evil, which is accompanied by an excuse, is the greatest force of destruction in the world" Unlike evil of the body, which stems from anger,

---

24 Aharon Shmuel Tamares, "Herut," in *Mussar Ha'Torah Veh'hayadut* (Vilna: Graber, 1912), 27–49.

jealousy, and other negative emotions, the evil of the intellect gains strength from the manipulation of political leaders. The evil of the body is individual and takes place covertly. In contrast, the evil of the intellect occurs publicly, and only when individuals separate themselves from society can they discern between the two.

The evil of slavery was a form of political evil based upon deceit, justified by Egypt according to necessity. The giving of the Torah, according to Rabbi Tamares, provided Jews with a task and presented them with the tools to implement it. The task of the Jew is to stand apart and identify the space of truth and of deceit. The Torah is the tool with which we determine the area of truth, according to Rabbi Tamares, while the modern space of deception is the state.

"This is the secret of all wars, activities, massacres, and mass killings in the world in general and of the persecution of Jews and pogroms in particular; the secret of the union of whole nations to attack and oppress weak nations." Murder is the worst sin, but the state presents killing in the context of war as a necessary action; this is the most evil form of violence.

Rabbi Tamares calls on us as Jews to honestly and critically examine the reality around us, and the excuses offered up by the state, not only by Israel but by every state. With Rabbi Tamares's challenge in mind, we return to the issue of Israel's control over the Palestinians. Does our freedom indeed depend upon the continuation of this control, as the state's leadership claims?

Defense as Prevention against Action Versus Defense as Prevention against Being

The idea that Palestinian freedom will harm our liberty and our lives stems from intellectual evil of deceitful origin. We are not occupiers because we must be occupiers. We are occupiers because *we are able to* be occupiers.

The laws in the Torah about someone who breaks into another person's home stipulate that a person is permitted to murder the robber if there is suspicion that they will kill first. In addition, there are laws in the Torah that a person is allowed, and indeed required, to kill someone who is attempting to kill somebody else; and, of course, a community is permitted to protect its members. But in all of these cases, self-defense means preventing some action that is already taking place. The halachic principle of "if somebody comes to kill you, kill them first" is not a call to violence as a way of life but an articulation of the permissibility of using violence to stop active violence. For example, in the eighth chapter of Mishnah Sanhedrin, we learn that the laws regarding killing a person attempting to kill another person require that the person trying to kill somebody else is told that the halachic punishment for such action is death. The laws surrounding killing a dangerous robber who breaks into the home stipulate that the robber must still be inside the house at the time of the killing. It is forbidden to kill a robber who is no longer inside the home, and it is prohibited to kill somebody who is not dangerous. In order to qualify as defense, an act must prevent another action as it is taking place.

The military control over Palestinians is not a temporary reality but a continuous one. The occupation does not prevent a specific action against us. It is a constant, violent phenomenon in our lives. Yet withholding freedom from other people out of a concern that they *might* use it against us is an ethical distortion. Our tradition does not allow continuous subjugation because we fear attack. Violence based on a hypothetical is radically un-Jewish.

Today, we have a hard time imagining, in our minds and in our hearts, an Israel that does not subjugate Palestinians. Those who demand Palestinian freedom are seen as traitors and as out of touch with reality. The Israeli ethos dictates that the country is not a temporary occupier but an eternal occupier, and this is Israel's essential nature. "The death of the two-state solution" is unquestionably accepted as fact.

In addition to the tremendous suffering that we cause to millions of people, this moral sin entails the creation of an internal contradiction in our ethical language. Our freedom is allegedly bound up with the subjugation of others. But how can freedom be a positive concept if our state exists only because it prevents others from freedom? How can we talk about social, economic, or gender equality when our state is based upon inequality?

There are those in our society who want to be ethical and yet believe that we need to deny Palestinians their freedom, while others in the Israeli community are no longer interested in ethics. For those who refuse to accept that our daily life must rely on the subjugation of others, the only option is a state of near constant blindness to that reality of oppression. This is especially true because we enjoy the fruits of occupation beyond the control it gives us, relishing the real estate and the cheap labor force it provides. Today, we use the subjugation of others for our own benefit and for our own comfort. We do not occupy because we need to; we occupy because we can. It is no surprise therefore that we take what we can.

Contentment is a fundamental attribute in our ethical literature. Our rabbis understood that amassing property and other capital can lead to ethical deterioration. In the case of Israel, the demand for more is accompanied by a severe yet baseless attempt to persuade us that this is the only way to live, that this is the proper way. Yet we are not protecting ourselves; we are instead enjoying the many things we have taken from those whose freedom we have denied.

I am confident that if we understood the price that millions of people must pay for our freedom, we would not be able to continue our lives as usual. We would not be able to function if we internalized our responsibility for hunger in Gaza or the fact that there are people in the South Hebron Hills without water or people in slave-like conditions picking dates in the Jordan Valley or that mothers and fathers are not safe in their homes in Hebron; if we understood the pain of tens of thousands of families divided by different residency statuses or the many thousands of people whose parents or children have been jailed for years in administrative detention; if we understood the feeling of parents who try to protect their children as their homes are broken into in the middle of the night for patrols, arrests, Shin Bet mapping exercises, or purely for training drills; if we could internalize that all of this happens directly because of us, not because it necessarily has to be so but because of our choice to use force,

It is our obligation as religious people to examine the reality around us and to ask how we, as religious people, ought to respond to it. Our first obligation is therefore to internalize the fact that the subjugation of Palestinians does not stem from necessity but from ability and desire. If we want to be Jews that respond to our tradition, we cannot base our lives on blindness and belligerence.

6

Listening

The virtue of seeing is important. Yet the virtue of hearing is greater because the power of hearing is purer and finer than the power of visibility.
—Bahya Ben Asher, *Kad HaKemach* (Spain, thirteenth century)[1]

The Letter, Part 3

Not long ago, it was a Friday, and I traveled with my daughter to see my brother in Haifa. He lives in an Arab neighborhood. I ask passersby how to get to his place, but no one knows where the address is. It's not so known among Jews. For over an hour, I wandered around and couldn't ask anyone. The girl and I are both tired, and we don't have the energy to keep walking. It's almost Shabbat. What do I do? An idea came to me. I'll go to the closest police station and ask there. I tell the officer the whole story, how I'd been wandering the neighborhood for more than an hour without finding my brother's address. The officer who heard my story immediately rose and brought a jeep from the garage, and soon after, I heard the sound of the engine. "Please, get in the car with the girl." The police officer drove us in the car to the door of my brother's house. I couldn't thank him properly. Then, with a hearty laugh and a Shabbat shalom, he disappeared with the car. Simcha, think how the heart expands with joy from an episode like this. The words "police officer" just yesterday brought us fear and trembling. We feared the words "police officer" so much that we couldn't sleep or eat, and here the police officer offered us such beautiful and warm hospitality, like our father, Abraham. Even if they are police officers, this is our State; this is our police. Ours for good and for bad. Its advantages and disadvantages. All of it, all of it is ours. Thus, I say every morning the prayer of Kalev ben Yefuneh and Yehoshua ben Nun: "May God save you from the counsel of spies." I do not

---

1 Bahya ben Asher, "Wandering of the Heart and Eye," in *Kad ha-Kemah* (New York: Kelilat Hayofi Publishinig, 1960), 80b.

want to write bad words about our holy land, which has barely awakened from her thousand years of slumber.

—Raanana Immigration Camp, July 25th, 1949 (written by my grandfather, Yechiel Mikhael Becher, upon his arrival in the Land of Israel in 1949, translated from Yiddish by Yael Levi)

I am on a train to Haifa and am rereading my grandfather's letter of excitement about a Jewish regime. "All of it is ours." But despite his feeling of ownership, his dream of the biblical forefathers and Mount Carmel, and his excitement about Jewish police forces, on that same Friday, my grandfather still wandered around an Arabic-speaking neighborhood and got lost. He got lost in an Arab neighborhood in Haifa because he did not understand the language of the native residents. In the Poland of old, he was native, yet the sight of a police officer made him tremble in fear. And here, in his land, he is a foreigner, yet the police officer calms him. And the native Arabic-speaking Arabs? Where are they in his story of return? There's no way to know. They are in his letter, but I cannot hear them.

As the years have passed, suspicion towards and ignorance of the native minority in Israel has turned into hatred. Today, the Arab community in Israel is treated as an actual enemy. People effectively consider their communal and national demands as incitement to violence and refer to their customs as terrorism. We have no interest in hearing them. I do not feel foreign in the Land of Israel, yet *I* sometimes get lost in Arab neighborhoods. I do not want to impose my authority to intimidate those in my surroundings in order to feel at home. But to avoid this, I must listen to those same voices that are so absent from my grandfather's letter.

Listening is a traditional religious virtue. Rabbi Yonah Gerondi, or Rabbeinu Yonah, who was also called the Hasid, writes about the value of listening in thirteenth-century Catalonia in his book *Shaarei Teshuva* (Section 2, 12):

> King Solomon, peace be upon him, also said [Proverbs 15]: "what brightens the eyes gladdens the heart, and good news fattens the bones. So the ear that heeds the reproof of life abides among the wise." And every wise-hearted person ought to know that it cannot be that King Solomon, peace be upon him, wrote these idle words for no reason [in the middle of] words of rebuke and fear of God because scripture has already testified about him that [1 Kings 5] "he was the wisest of all men." Rather, this

is the meaning of the matter. What brightens the eyes gladdens the heart. So the eye is an esteemed organ because one sees the light that gladdens the heart through it. But more esteemed is the ear because, through it, one will hear good news which fattens the bones, for it has no feeling and will not be fattened from the light of the eyes unless it is an extra enjoyment. And so did they of blessed memory say that the ear is more esteemed than the other organs. For if one blinded someone's eye, he must pay the value of the eye, but if one made someone deaf, he must pay his full value. And indeed, a person is obligated to serve our blessed God with all of his organs because they were created to serve God, as it says [Proverbs 16]: "God made everything for God's purpose." Therefore, even with the esteemed limbs God made in him, he is obligated to worship their maker. And a great punishment is even much greater if one prevents them from doing God's commandments; he does not perform the service with them and does not reciprocate with them. Because God did a great kindness with him through his esteemed senses and crowned him with honor and glory through them.

I am traveling to Haifa, but not to search for my grandfather's brother's house. Instead, I am here to complete part of my grandfather's story, which is also part of my story as a religious person in the State of Israel. Much of the Jewish population thinks it doesn't need to listen to the accounts of Arabs. Listening is seen as self-erasure or even betrayal. But our tradition teaches us that it is, in fact, a lack of listening that stands in opposition to God's will, which requires that we use the tools we have, use our whole selves, to be better Jews. "A person is obligated to serve our blessed God with all of his organs," Rabbi Gerondi writes. I am traveling to meet Samer Swaid, a friend and political partner, to listen to him. We have a lot in common. Politically, we see eye to eye on many topics. We have both been politically active for most of our adult lives. But we are also very different. Samer is secular, and I am religious. He is a member of a minority group, and I am part of the majority.

Samer is a Palestinian Arab from the Druze community. He is active in the socialist Hadash party as a member of its national leadership. He is the executive director of the Arab Center for Alternative Planning. The State of Israel confiscated almost all of the land of Peki'in, Samer's home village, and gave it to Jewish towns. Samer is a threefold minority. He is an Arab citizen within a Jewish majority; he is a Druze minority within an Arab population, which is majority Muslim; and he is a political minority within the Druze community because he chooses to identify as "Palestinian"—meaning that he emphasizes his native Palestinian nationalism, unlike many Druze who reject this identity.

In Haifa, we sit for breakfast in a café downtown. I wonder whether this is the neighborhood where my grandfather searched for his brother on a Friday afternoon seventy years ago.

Samer is the kind of person who, when he talks, makes silence envelop a room. He chooses his words carefully and speaks quietly and confidently.

[...]

"Listen, the Druze were never really given a chance to be Jews, so it's impossible for them to integrate into the State of Israel fully. The historical process that the Druze experienced before and after the founding of the state [...] gives the impression that there was an opportunity for integration, but that isn't true. But first, I'll share some background:

"We Druze are part of the Palestinian milieu, and therefore, in my view, there's not a question of whether Druze are Palestinians or not. Just like in Lebanon, the Druze are Lebanese, without any qualifications, and so too in Syria; the Druze here are part of the native Palestinian milieu. That cannot be erased. This isn't just my opinion; it is also expressed in our language.

"For example, in groups of religious leaders that we share, Syrians and Lebanese [...] call us 'the Druze of Palestine.' Everyone accepts this, including Sheikh Moafaq Tarif, the spiritual leader of Druze in Israel and also connected to the State of Israel bureaucratically. Druze from other countries call us Palestinian, and he and everyone else accepts this. No Druze from the Middle East says 'the Druze of Israel.' The geographical identity is Palestinian because that is the indigenous area here. For us, too, it has taken and continues to take time to understand this aspect of our identity.

"I call myself Palestinian because it conveys my indigenous identity. Because of this, I think that Druze are Palestinian. Today, I identify more with the Palestinian sphere than the Arab sphere. It better represents who I am.

"When I say to Druze people that I am Palestinian from a political identity perspective, and not only from a geographical perspective, it is not always warmly received. But everyone accepts that they are Arabs. This, however, is precisely what seems like a distortion to me. Because Arabness is not part of our Druze culture, it is specifically the indigenous component that is more logical here. Still, because of the 'Israelification' process, people see Palestinianness as something distant.

[...]

"See, in general, Palestinian political identity is complicated, and it's changed and continues to change. It's changing not just among Druze but among all minorities in Israel. Arabs in Israel, not just Druze in particular, underwent and are changing their political-national identities. We Arabs are undergoing a process of Palestinianization, which began in the First Intifada and has continued even more powerfully since the Oslo process. This is a phenomenon that did not start with the foundation of the state. This collective identity gained strength in particular after Oslo because we suddenly doubted the understanding of this space. Firstly, we did this because it became less dangerous to talk about Palestinian identity within Israel. Less persecution by the Shabak (Israel security agency) and that sort of thing. But there was another reason. During the negotiations of the 90's, the Arabs in Israel weren't counted. We remained outside the picture. No one talked about Palestinians who were citizens of Israel, neither the PLO nor Rabin. No one talked about us and asked about our status after a solution was achieved. And then we started to feel that we needed to prove that we Arabs exist to the Palestinian people and the State of Israel. We are not an immigrant minority but a native minority; we began to talk about our identity as a native identity. This happened both in the political parties and also in the Arab mainstream.

"But the Druze are a more complicated case than other Arabs in Israel. Why? Not because we underwent integration into the Jewish Israel milieu but because we were part of it differently from other Arab citizens. I need to emphasize that just because we didn't undergo the same process of 'Palestinianization' that Muslims did doesn't mean that we underwent a process of 'Israelization.' Unlike Arab Muslims or Christians, our process concerning Jews was different, and our culture is also different. We have a different culture. Unlike others, we closed ourselves off as a religious group. We learned about and came to understand the relevant powers in the space and tried to make do physically and religiously here, with an understanding that we need to preserve ourselves as a minority.

"This generally characterizes the Druze, not only in relationship with the state. The community of the Druze people is the central element representing our identity; this is our primary identity. The central institution is the family and the chain of transmission. Regarding marriages, you only marry a Druze woman, even if you are staunchly secular—it's not something that is challenged under any circumstances. Even if you are cut off from Druze society and live in a place where there are no Druze, you'll seek out a Druze woman to marry. So we identify ourselves collectively differently, which influences how we interface with the state. There are religious reasons for this, but also, of course, historical reasons.

[...]

"From a religious perspective, from the day we were established, we have been under persecution. We developed in a place with a Muslim majority. We grew down in Cairo some thousand years ago, where there was Muslim hegemony. Not only that, but we were an outgrowth of Islam and opposed it. Like any group from a different religion, you can imagine that the other religion doesn't see it so favorably that we heretically deny everything they say and believe in.

"So the Druze always tried to preserve themselves relatively closed off. How do you preserve yourself? For example, there is a principle called *taqiya*. It states that when you, as a Druze person, are with people who are not Druze, you do not need to accentuate what differentiates you but rather what is similar between you because you are a minority. You don't have the power to fight the majority. Also, there's the matter of family and marriage. We stay inside the community.

"But you have to understand, closing ourselves off isn't an apolitical matter. First of all, Druze acted and continued to act as a national group. Our history is complicated, like everyone's, and it also contains issues of politics and power relations. Many don't know this, but there was once a Druze state. There were Druze emirates whose center was in Lebanon. It reached all the way to Mount Carmel. The emirates even transferred Druze communities people to Carmel hills. The Druze people living in Daliyat al-Karmel and Isfiya originated in Syria. There was no religious significance to the emirates. They were political emirates with good relations with the relevant powers in Istanbul. We also have a history of resistance. There were national Druze rebellions. The Druze led the massive Arab Revolt against the French mandate in Syria. This was at the beginning of the twentieth century. It was an explicitly Druze pan-Arab attempt, and it succeeded. And also, in the rebellion against the Brits, the Druze took part. We are a religious people, but you can't confuse religiosity, even religious closed-off-ness, with being apolitical.

[...]

"As I said, the Druze developed differently in Israel. During the Arab Revolt of 1936, we had a unique place that influenced our relations with the Zionists. When the Arab rebels' power weakened throughout the rebellion, the rebels looked for ways to strengthen themselves. So the insurgents would enter and take over villages and use the village's resources. So naturally, hostility developed between the Arab farmers and the rebel leadership. For example, the rebels would approach a village head and ask to slaughter sheep for food for the rebels. But the food belonged to the villagers. So hostility began among the Druze. Because the rebel leadership was Muslim and there was a religious side to the revolt, they started to feel that they were outside the struggle. Add to this the fact that there wasn't a Druze elite in the same way that there was a Christian elite. So unsurprisingly, they began to connect with the Zionist movement, which also had an interest in weakening the revolt.

"Perhaps the starkest expression of this was that there was a member of the Knesset from a bloc party of Mapai in the '50s by the name of Salah Hanifes. His father was one of the leaders of the Arab Revolt against the Zionists. His father was executed in an internal leadership conflict. He harbored resentment against the Muslim rebel leadership. The Zionist movement knew how to enter and create divisions in leadership. The mandate also learned how to do this.

"But the connection between Jews and Druze was never unequivocal. Even when relationships between Druze and Zionists developed, it didn't prevent the fact that in the 1948 War, Druze took part on the Arab side. A battle next to Shfaram of a fully Druze unit fought against the Haganah.

"For all these reasons, it's hard to talk about our assimilation into Jewish society. Instead, I would prefer to think of ourselves as a minority community that developed differently, in different and sometimes conflicting ways.

[...]

"And within all of this is the religious aspect. We are, of course, also a religious group. Our religion is also political. Every religion has an ideological element to it. For example, a Druze person remains Druze when reincarnated, and we must preserve ourselves, so it is forbidden to assimilate. It's not permitted to marry someone who isn't Druze. Even if someone is killed, fate is accepted to a great degree. We do not sanctify death. We do not have martyrdom. There's an acceptance in the sense that you continue to the next incarnation. These things are ideological, ethical, and political and construct an ethics between a person and the community.

"Because I am not religious, I prefer not to talk too much about the whole matter of redemption. We don't talk about religion to outsiders. But there is undoubtedly a moment of redemption. And that has implications for how to behave in this life. There's a daily order. There are restrictions, for example drinking alcohol, and there are holidays. All of this is ethics.

[...]

"So where am I in all of this? My father, of blessed memory, was a communist. He died when I was eight. So my mother was left with eight children when she was thirty-seven. I am the fifth. We're talking about a family [...], let's say my mother worried about how to survive. The family wasn't engaged in politics, but a family tradition was that my father was a communist. Party members would visit our home; it was part of my childhood and community. The party was strong in our village, which is how my father had become a communist. He was a communist in the classical sense; he was a worker and believed that the means of production belonged to us, this whole business. In my adolescence, I started to study him, and I got my political understanding from him.

"But I must note that my community doesn't represent all Druze communities. The party had a robust presence, and there were always party events. There were always panels; that was the public atmosphere. It was, therefore, easy for me to continue my father's path early. My mother is like every older Druze woman, who becomes religious at a certain stage in her life. So she wasn't communist in the sense of negating religion. Still, from her perspective, she identified with communism from the perspective of class relations and identifying with the position of Arabs who want peace and equality within Israel.

"My siblings aren't activists. They vote Hadash not only because of me but because of the tradition. So the religious motives came from home, and the leftist motives came from home. In Druze society, there isn't a difference or rifts within the community. In the same house, you'll find everything. Some time ago, a well-known Druze singer died in the village of Yirka, who was a communist. He had been a security prisoner for a period. But his oldest son was a well-known religious figure. So this religious figure welcomed those who came to comfort them, including communists, and we didn't think this was strange or exceptional. We know how to live together in peace, at least for now. But in my opinion, it won't last long. Modern is entering our communities, and religious figures are tightening their belts.

[. . .]

"Three of my siblings didn't go to the army, and one did. When he served in the military, he did the minimum and got some position guarding a base somewhere.

"I refused. Okay, I'll explain. My refusal wasn't on clearly ideological grounds. I went to the army's induction center and said I didn't want to enlist. They said, 'you have a ninety-seven profile [the score given to those who are fit for combat duty]; you're going to the Druze combat unit.' I said okay, and then I left and ran home. I didn't say, 'I refuse on principle.' But they caught me and put me on trial, and that began a saga where I was constantly in and out of jail. Finally, after a year and a bit, someone came to me, the 'head of the Minorities Department,' who was Druze himself, and offered me a deal. He said that I couldn't be released, and I'm just accumulating more time in the system, and it's a shame. He said that with service of half a year, on a base close to home, they would cancel all of my fines and shorten my service. I thought about it and said okay. And I did half a year. And then I got out. I had a social life in the army and didn't try to distance myself forcibly. I wasn't on an anti-army campaign. I simply didn't want to be there. It wasn't a statement. In the end, I served in Haifa, right here. And they kept their word and canceled the rest for me. The department head checked the box that another Druze had served, and from my perspective, I got to check the box for myself too because I wanted to do as little as possible in this system.

"So. Therefore, I don't tell myself that I was a refusenik. I wore a uniform for a period. By the way, I sometimes get attacked for this. But it's part of my past. Just like my political past. In the village, I was always politically involved on the local level. I remember that I was at the protest where Rabin was murdered. As a fifteen-year-old kid. In the 1999 elections (ironically, when I was between rounds of military jail), I was very involved in the campaign for Ehud Barak.

"But all of this changed after I was released. In 2001, I started university. This was a period of a lot of political activity. I was busy with my studies, and I also worked all sorts of construction jobs and that sort of thing. But I joined the Hadash student group on campus and suddenly became very active. And then I thought to myself: I want to challenge Hadash. Will they let a Druze be the head of the committee? They did. Not only did they allow it, but I was the trump card because all the Druze voted for me, no matter their political background. This says something about Hadash but also about the Druze. I don't know; maybe it's a bit unfortunate but also meaningful, this sort of community and fraternity. In any case, it's not superficial. I remember seeing two Druze lieutenant colonels in line to vote for Hadash because I was the representative. They didn't even know me, but I'm Druze.

"And then, from this, I started to become active. In 2003, I ran for the National Secretariat as the youth representative, then I was elected first among the youth, and since then, I've been on the secretariat. After that, I started to work in the Knesset for Hana Sweid, to whom I'm not related and is actually a Christian. I note this because you all ask me this all the time.

"I also became active in other areas. There's a military refusal council for Druze, and I was the secretary. From 2009 until 2011, I helped people who decided to refuse. At that time, I wanted to write a thesis on Druze refusal, but it didn't happen in the end. It's definitely something that interests me. The motivation to serve interests me. It's not an ideological motivation but material. It's an understanding of how one integrates into society.

"There, too, the Druze are changing. After the Nation-State Law, they stopped talking about a covenant sealed in blood but rather a covenant of life. There's anger towards the state, but we're talking about a long process. There's also a structural issue of where we will find Druze power.

[...]

"There's no developed Druze civil society. There's an Israeli civil society that has branches in Druze communities. The big foundations, like the Rashi Foundation and the American Jewish Joint Distribution Committee. There are very few local initiatives in the sense of local groups, and they generally don't survive.

"On the other hand, there are many charity projects among Druze. There are people in need, and we take care of them in our geographical community and the whole Druze community.

"During the war in Syria, Druze in Israel donated millions of dollars. I live in a community of four thousand Druze. Not long ago, there was a donation drive, and I remember that people donated more than two hundred thousand dollars during a single week. The same thing happened when there was the war in Lebanon. Because even when there isn't a daily connection, there are familial and national connections. My grandmother is Lebanese, so even if I'm not familiar with it personally, and even if we can't visit one another, there's a feeling of belonging.

"I know the family a little; the Lebanese are engineers in the Gulf, but there's a problem with meeting in Jordan, and they also have a problem meeting with Israelis, and I can understand that. But it's more than a family connection. I have no connection to Syria, but it was important to me to donate there. It was also important to me to donate to Palestinians in Gaza who aren't Druze.

[...]

"There's no doubt that my situation vis-à-vis Israeliness has changed. I try to be pragmatic and speak with Jewish Israeli society. I also once thought there was no need to emphasize an 'oppositional' identity, but I no longer believe that today. But my erasure has increased in recent times. It also influences how we see you Jews. And how we see the state. I don't see Palestinians who are citizens of Israel distinguishing between Israelis and Jews. I also see them as the same. You all think that everything is yours.

"This is how I see you all: what is vital to Israeli Jews is to remain hegemonic, even if they need to walk all over me for it. That's what's most important to them. They want me to be a good Arab who will accept their hegemony. It's expressed in every daily interaction. In my work, when I cooperate with Jewish organizations, I know where the realm of cooperation is and where it stops. And if in my organization—I run a project on displaced villages and land—I won't mention it just anywhere because it threatens Jews. One of my understandings of Palestinian discourse in Israel is that our discourse can be more effective. We don't take into account your fears, those of the majority. The fear is of losing control. What's strange is that we don't even have a goal to be the majority and rule. It's an imagined threat, and you live in fear of it.

"Once, Jamal Zahalka said in a speech in the Knesset that we were here before you, and we will be here after you. It was an unnecessary statement. We have no goal of expelling you. I don't know; maybe because you were a minority in other places in the world, you need this. But that doesn't interest me so much. You attempt to preserve this because you are afraid, but also because it serves you. And because you can maintain it. The majority is always careful to tell me that they fear a demographic boundary, even though I have no interest in crossing that boundary.

"In Peki'in, the village where I was born, there are Jews. There always were, long before Zionism. I come from such a place. A person can be both Arab and Jewish. In my view, I don't want to be a Druze majority, and it's not essential to me that there be a Druze majority. I want to be in a place where an egalitarian majority accepts one another. I want the majority to be similar to me from an ethical perspective, not an ethnic identity perspective. I acknowledge and accept that the majority is Jewish, but I want a moral majority on matters of principle.

[...]

"I believe that if there will be peace, it will also be good for the Palestinian citizens of Israel, even if we are not an active part of the process. I think that it will lead to a change in perspective. It's hard to intimidate people when you live in peace. It doesn't take hold; it doesn't work. I know that this is a discourse on some parts of the left, the matter of being cautious of peace. But to change the existing hegemony, we need peace.

"Listen, anyone who wants to replace the right-wing needs to include Arabs. If that happens, we will create real change here. We're building on this. You and I—we're indeed political people.

"I believe my role here as a Palestinian minority can be very positive. We don't only need to be different from you; we can also be a bridge. We can empower both sides and, along the way, empower ourselves.

"Because what's your problem? What's your real problem? That you never thought about what it means to integrate here. You thought to be here as some sort of strange flavor in the Middle East. The perpetual war contributes to this. As soon as this situation is solved and you feel that you're not at war, you also won't need to always think about group isolation. You won't be threatened. When peace comes, the culture will also change. Now you see the Western world, so you celebrate Valentine's Day and all those holidays. You'll also see us when you're not at war with us. You'll also feel freer to celebrate the Muslim Feast of Sacrifice.

[...]

"I think the Druze group is the most disadvantaged in Israel. You expropriated the land of all the Arabs. But with us, you also expropriated our identity and values that you didn't claim from others. And it affected how we acted. The Arab left also needs to deal with this. We also need to make space for the Druze.

"And here, you also have a role. You Jews have much more power and hegemony that wants equality than you think. You need to believe in yourselves more and internalize how much power you have. You are afraid of the results of what you say. You are fearful of offering an alternative. So you make life easy for yourselves.

"For years already, I've thought that one of the reasons that 'the two-state solution is unsuccessful with the public has to do with the fact that its prominent public representatives don't truly believe in it. They want approximately two states, but always to still preserve a bit of power in any case, a bit of control, a bit too much territory."

Epilogue

My grandfather wore a *gartel* whenever he prayed. So about two years ago, in an attempt to get to know my grandfather's religious world, I also started to wear a gartel when I pray. A gartel is a sort of belt. You wrap a black rope around your waist at the beginning of prayer before putting on a tallit (prayer shawl) and tefillin (phylacteries). Every Hasidic court has its type of gartel—some are thick, and some are thin and rounded. Members of some courts wear the gartel all day, while others only wear it when praying or studying Torah. Some only allow a married man to wear the gartel, while some permit it before marriage. In a world where every detail symbolizes different ways of communicating with God, even the number of strings that make up the gartel has mystical meanings.

The source for the custom of putting on a belt before praying appears in the Talmud (Brachot 24b) but was formalized by the Hasidim. The goal of the belt is to separate between the heart and the genitalia during prayer, "so that his heart shall not see his genitalia."

We need barriers that will distinguish between us and our impulses. Our ability to examine the state and society is strengthened when we see it from the outside. My freedom as an individual is dependent, among other things, on separation from the physical world of power around me. The mixing of worlds and blurring of boundaries constrains my freedom and subordinates my world of Torah to the world around me. During prayer, when we are in touch with God, we must be different people. We must separate from the world around us and return to the world of Torah.

When I started wearing the gartel, it brought me back in my memories to the moment I profaned God's name in the village of Salim. When I didn't remember before whom I stood, I was naked in front of the suffering and danger that I had caused. I was uncouth and subjugated to the power that I held in my hands. The requirement for gentleness is the requirement that comes together with thought, with my contemplation of the general reality and remembrance of the obligation cast upon me to be faithful to the tradition of my ancestors.

The Jewish world has changed significantly in the last hundred years. Specifically, in the realm of power and independence, there is a double force to the obligations we hold, to remember that we may not be uncouth. We may not sink into the numbness of the senses characteristic of those in power. The traditional world allows and requires upliftment; it allows and requires anticipating full redemption. It allows faith. Therefore, the first step is to separate from the logic of those with power.

Index

Milton Keynes UK
Ingram Content Group UK Ltd.
UKHW052047270324
440206UK00008B/626